How to
Use Images

How to
Use Images

Lindsey Marshall and Lester Meachem

Laurence King Publishing

LAURENCE KING

Published in 2010 by Laurence King Publishing Ltd
361–373 City Road
London EC1V 1LR
United Kingdom
Tel: + 44 20 7841 6900
Fax: + 44 20 7841 6910
e-mail: enquiries@laurenceking.com
www.laurenceking.com

A catalogue record for this book is available from the British Library

ISBN: 978-1-85669-658-6

Design: Studio Ten and a Half
Typeface: Helvetica
Picture Research: Carol Cooper and Peter Kent
Cover Picture Research: Miguel Laverde
Senior Editor: Sophie Page
Printed in China

Front cover: © ADAGP, Paris and DACS, London 2009

Related study material is available on the Laurence King
website at www.laurenceking.com

Contents

Introduction

This book is a creative, informative and practical introduction to the use of images for both print and screen. It provides a working knowledge of how to select and use images for a range of applications and contexts and is also a source of inspiration and reference.

It may be read sequentially or can be dipped into: each chapter, although relating to previous and following chapters, is structured to be read independently. The chapters cover who images are aimed at; why, when and how they are used; selecting images; how to structure a design; composition; communication; the use of colour; maximizing image potential; and production. However, before these practical issues are discussed, it is worthwhile taking a brief look at the history and background of how images have been used in the past as this informs current practice.

Opposite: Anna Francescutti's image shows a quirky and innovative approach to image generation.

❶ Top, left: this is an image of pictograms drawn on a cave wall thousands of years ago. Most of the images are easily identifiable as human or animal.

Bottom, left: Egyptian hieroglyphs, which are stylized pictures of objects representing syllables or sounds.

Top, right: medieval illuminated manuscript showing the use of images to illustrate the text, as well as for decoration.

History and Background

Images have been used as a means of communication throughout human history. Some of the earliest examples are found in caves, such as the dramatic large paintings in the Lascaux caves in France which date from 15,000 to 10,000 BC. Images were initially the basis for all communication but were gradually replaced with alphabets and similar written devices as societies became more sophisticated and the need for more complex communication arose. Even as images were replaced with text, they continued to form an important part of communication, as they still do today. The texts in early medieval manuscripts, for example, were illustrated with images to aid understanding. Because most people were illiterate, the person reading the text showed the illustrations to them as he read it, and also used the images as prompts when giving a sermon based on a manuscript. Parallel cultures developed different methods of communication but images have always been important; some, such as Egyptian hieroglyphs, incorporated abstract and stylized representations of objects. ❶

Pictograms, which are images that represent an object, also formed the basis of much communication, as did ideograms – images or symbols that represent a concept or action, and convey an abstract notion rather than depicting an object. Pictograms and ideograms are familiar images today, although they may differ between cultures. ❷

Communication and the use of images was revolutionized in the fifteenth century with the invention of the printing press, which enabled the mass production of type and images. Prior to this, certainly in Western countries, type and images were either reproduced by hand-lettering and illustration or by woodcut prints, which were time consuming to produce. Another technological development that made the consumption of images more widespread in the fifteenth century was the introduction of copperplate printing that enabled realistic and detailed images to be reproduced on a large scale. Many other technological developments have enabled different and better ways of producing images, not least of which are the halftone screen and photography. These have culminated in the recent and rapid developments in digital image and text production. ❸

❷ This image could be interpreted as a pictogram representing a bicycle or as an ideogram representing a cycleway or place where people can ride bicycles.

This shows two pictograms representing a man and a woman. The arrow turns the image into an ideogram for male and female lavatories.

❸ Woodcut of the prioress from Chaucer's *The Canterbury Tales*, printed in the 15ᵗʰ century.

Which Professions Use Images?

The increased availability of digital images, and the ease of creating your own, means that images are used in a range of professions. As well as the more obvious uses, such as in editorial, web, information, product and textile design, images are also used in professions such as archaeology, the law (for example, as evidence), marketing, advertising, architecture and education. Many people, such as account managers, use images to enhance or help in the interpretation of presentations.

Who Are the Intended Viewers/Readers?

This stencilled graffiti image suggests that communism (represented by the hammer and sickle) should be abandoned, but it is not clear as to what would replace it.

Although it may seem obvious, it is worth remembering that images are aimed at people and, as such, are subject to misinterpretation and misunderstanding. There are many different cultures, languages and visual languages, and it is therefore important to select images appropriate to the message to be communicated and the audience to be reached. This is discussed further in Chapter 4.

Why Are Images Used?

Images often replace or support text, and can also be used to grab the reader's attention. Examples include the use of celebrity images in magazines, or bold or shocking images in propaganda or advertising.

As well as replacing or supporting text, images are used to persuade or instruct. Advertising relies heavily on their use to persuade the public to purchase products or services. This is because images can be interpreted and understood quickly, whereas words take longer to digest. If you look at hoardings, magazines and newspapers, and at web sites and television, you will see that not much advertising design is text-based. The use of images provides the flexibility to communicate to a broader range of people and opens up more possibilities for the designer. The same image can be used in different ways: a single rose could be used to persuade in an advertisement for a florist or to instruct by providing information about the structure of the flower. Information graphics are usually enhanced by images as, in most cases, in a similar way to their use in persuasion, they can be more easily understood than text, without the need for translation. ❶

Images are powerful aids in helping people to understand instructions. We all know of examples, whether they are how to insert eye drops or more complex problems such as assembling flat-pack furniture. They are also used as educational aids or for reference: medical photographs, for example, can help with the identification of certain diseases or problems. ❷

In addition to persuasion and instruction, images can be used for various purposes, such as to guide readers, tell stories and express concepts. They may also illustrate a point made in the text or convey an emotion or action, for example, by using an image of a boot to indicate violence or aggression. They can also be used to supplement text, or provide a visual break between sections of text – or they can be the primary means of communication, as in many comics or children's picture books. Most design, however, is not purely image-based; a combination of image and text, designed to work together, forms the basis for most visual communication. ❸

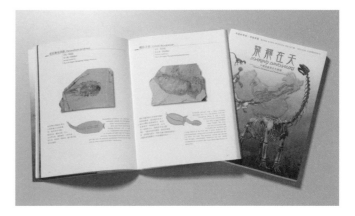

❶ This timetable and poster show the use of the same image for different purposes. In the first instance, the image of the bus is used to inform the reader of the timetable's content, and to link it to the advertisement in which the bus is used to promote the company's services.

❷ In this double-page spread Nicola Chang has used photographs of fossils with diagrams of what the fossilized creatures would have looked like originally in order to provide more detailed information.

❸ In this image Luke Coker has used the sole of a boot apparently coming out of the poster to represent violence. Luke produced this image as part of his degree portfolio and it does not represent the views and opinions of the charity featured.

Activity

Decide on a fairly simple activity, such as growing a plant from seed or putting a plug on an electrical appliance and, using images only (no words), make a series of diagrams/ pictures describing how to do this activity in a similar way to the examples shown below.

How to use the stamp

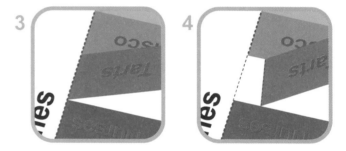

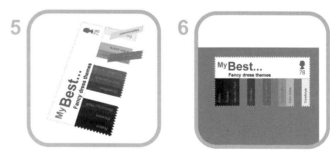

Matthew Day has used a series of images in order to demonstrate how to use his tear-off stamp design.

Where Are Images Used?

Images are used everywhere in our daily lives, often without us being conscious of them. Like good typography, good use of images may often go unnoticed. However, there are often occasions where images would be ineffectual if they weren't noticed, when they are used for their shock value, as in the example shown. ❶

In an average day we consume thousands of images, all used in different ways and for different purposes. While shopping we encounter images used in packaging, logos, labelling, signage, window displays, web pages, brochures, hoardings, posters and point-of-purchase displays. This is without the television, magazine or web site advertisements that may have prompted the shopping spree in the first place.

Images are often used as visual prompts or signposts; in furniture catalogues, for instance, products are shown in a real domestic situation with people using them to suggest their use and how they would improve the reader's lifestyle. This is particularly the case in web design where, with increased access to software, images and moving images are central to communication. As people browse the pages, images provide a hook, persuading them to continue browsing and drawing them in. ❷

What might Darfur be losing in terms of history when a village is burned and destroyed?

The loss is staggering. The destruction of old constructions like mosques, the graves of the Fur sultans in Jebel Marra, traditional items such as holy drums, the fine clothes of traditional leaders and written documents like hawakir documents which prove land possession, is irretrievable. A village, an entire oral history, is suddenly wiped off the face of the earth as if it never existed.

What kind of animals are typically kept in the village?

Often it is donkeys and goats. Wealthier families may also keep sheep. Pastoralists have cows, mainly in South Darfur, and camels, mainly in North Darfur. In some satellite images, it is possible to discern herds of cattle near villages.

What significance do these animals have for a village's livelihood?

For poorer families, these animals represent their entire wealth. Since the conflict began, productivity has spiraled downwards - in terms of both farming and livestock production. Livestock trade has collapsed. The multiple attacks of government forces and other armed militias have amounted to the systematic destruction of livelihoods and livelihood systems.

What happens to livestock during an attack on a village by armed groups?

Often the livestock is stolen. Less frequently, because of their value, the animals are killed and/or mutilated. Donkeys are often killed - sometimes simply because they were tied up at the time of the attack, other times because they are not valued by people, especially by the Janjawid militias, who place a high value on camels and horses.

Dead donkey – left tied up during attack on Tiero, Chad.

photo: UNHCR

❶ This screenshot from an Amnesty International web site uses shocking images to alert people to the horror of what is happening in some countries.

❷ In this page from a furnishings catalogue, the products are shown in use, with an action shot of a child using the chair as the central image.

This series of screenshots from the Petit Carnet web site demonstrate the effective use of image to draw the reader in and maintain interest in the site but, at the same time, create variety.

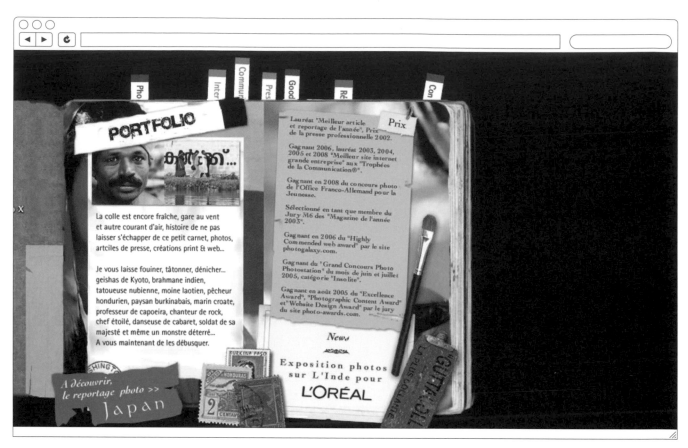

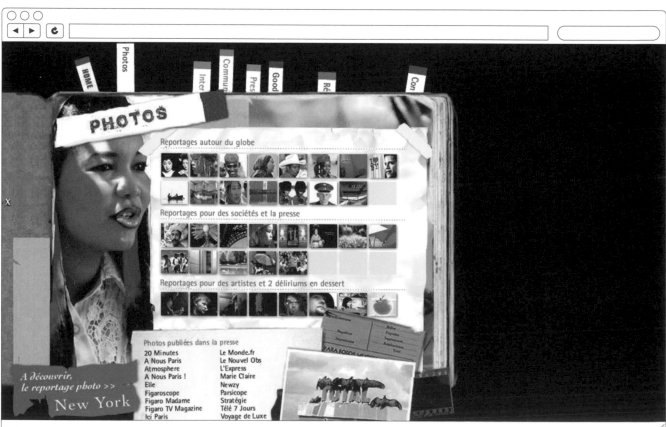

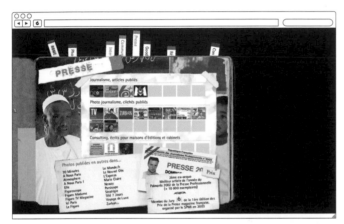

❶ An example of the use of image as
the main means of communication is
this web site, which is about forestry.
Pop-up information and explanations
also rely on image.

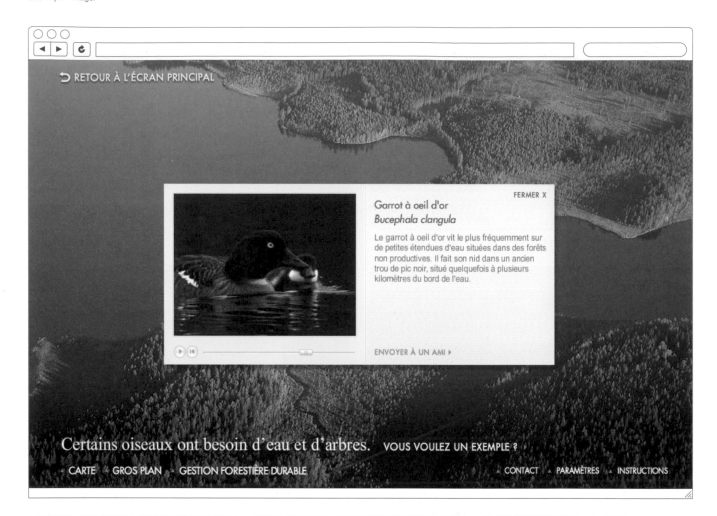

When Are Images Used?

Images can be a useful replacement or support for words. If you are trying to persuade someone to buy a dress, a picture of a model looking good in the dress is far more powerful than any number of eloquently written descriptions, or even an image of the dress laid flat or on a mannequin.

Images are also particularly useful when it's necessary to get information across quickly, as they can act as abbreviations or shorthand. Images used in this way can, in many but not all instances, reach a broader audience. This can be seen at airports where international symbols are used for information signage.

An image is often the starting point for communication, as on the front cover of a book or magazine. It may be the subject of the communication itself, such as in a birdwatcher's book where the image of the bird is the primary method of identification, supplemented by descriptive text. ❶ ❷

Sometimes, images are the only way to communicate a message. This is often the case with warning signs where a sense of urgency and clarity is required. ❸

Images are used in a similar way as tools for teaching in language textbooks, or as visual aids where a description may be confusing. A good example of the latter is found in 'point to it' books where images of everyday objects are shown to help communication when there is a language barrier. ❹

There are other considerations as to why, when and how images are used. These include the target audience, the way an image will contribute to the overall design, what purpose the image serves other than decoration and, most importantly, what the message is. All these issues will be discussed in the chapters that follow. The exciting thing about images is that, although they are ubiquitous, they still provide designers with creative opportunities each time they consider a graphic or web design project or problem.

TONY HERTZ *Megalaureatum Radiopassionis*

Especie: Creativo y propietario de agencia de publicidad en radio. Hábitat: Birmingham. Distribución: Reino Unido, EE.UU., Francia, Japón...

Species: Creative and radio companies owner. Habitat: Birmingham. Distribution: UK, USA, France, Japan...

♂

La pasión desaforada de Tony Hertz por la radio se ha dilatado a lo largo y ancho de 30 años, cuatro continentes y una trayectoria profesional como director creativo y propietario de empresas de radio. En 2001 creó Hertz: Radio tras 14 años trabajando en McCann-Erickson en Japón, Bélgica y el Reino Unido. Antes de McCann, su empresa de Londres, The Radio Operators, cubrió paredes enteras de certificados y objetos de extraño diseño, como premios Clio, Gold y Silver ILR, London International, D&AD Silver y el primer D&AD radio Gold de la historia. Este año dirige en Cannes el workshop Radio for Art Directors.

Tony Hertz's passion-beyond-all-reason for radio has spanned 30 years, four continents and careers as an agency creative director, and proprietor of his own radio companies. He launched Hertz:Radio in 2001, after 14 years as a Creative Director at McCann-Erickson in Japan, Belgium and the UK, winning radio awards in all three places. Before McCann, Tony's company in London, The Radio Operators, amassed walls full of certificates and oddly shaped objects including Clio, Gold and Silver ILR Awards, London International, D&AD Silver and the first ever D&AD radio Gold. Radio for Art Directors will be a featured workshop at the 2006 Cannes Lions.

WORKSHOP

La radio para directores de arte

Impartiré el workshop La radio para directores de arte, con un contenido valioso para directores de arte y diseñadores: cómo encontrar ideas eficaces para el medio radiofónico; cómo adaptar conceptos que ya han funcionado en TV y gráfica; cómo usar música y efectos de sonido; cómo presentar campañas de radio al cliente; cómo llevar a cabo un casting o la selección de un estudio de radio.

Radio for Art Directors

He will offer a great workshop called Radio for Art Directors, with a valuable content for design professionals: how to find efficient ideas for radio advertising, how to adapt those concepts that have worked well on paper and TV, how to use music and sound effects, how to present radio campaigns to clients, and how to run a casting or a radio studio election.

☐ Conferencia / Conference: 06/07/06, 18h   ☐ Workshop: 06/07/06, 10-13h

❷ In this design, Astrid Stavro has used the picture of the bird as the main means of communication because the page is about the bird. The rest of the content supports and supplements the image.

❸ This sign relies on a strong image to communicate that there is a danger of death without relying on the words, which may not be understood.

❹ An example of the use of image as a teaching aid is in children's books where an image of the item is positioned next to the word and reinforces the letter of the alphabet.

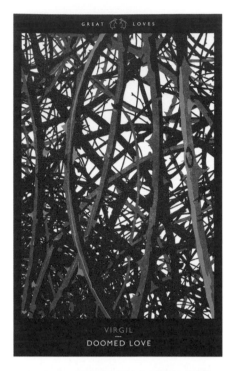

GREAT LOVES

VIRGIL
—
DOOMED LOVE

GREAT LOVES

FROM THE LETTERS OF ABELARD AND HELOISE
—
FORBIDDEN FRUIT

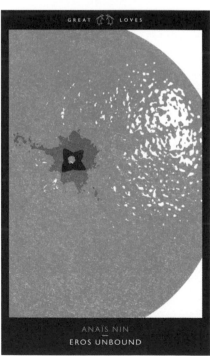

GREAT LOVES

GIACOMO CASANOVA
—
OF MISTRESSES, TIGRESSES AND OTHER CONQUESTS

GREAT LOVES

SØREN KIERKEGAARD
—
THE SEDUCER'S DIARY

GREAT LOVES

IVAN TURGENEV
—
FIRST LOVE

GREAT LOVES

ANAÏS NIN
—
EROS UNBOUND

Selection

1

Whatever purpose an image is used for, there is normally a process of selecting the one that is most appropriate for the job. This can mean choosing from a range of available images or deciding on the sort of image required and either sourcing it or arranging for it to be produced/photographed. In order to do this, it is important to understand the various ways in which images are produced and where they can be found.

Before you get to this stage in the process, you will need an understanding of the intended audience and the meanings associated with, for example, symbols.

Other factors not to be overlooked when selecting images include social and legal issues and the need, with some exceptions, to credit the author, artist or designer of any material that is used.

Opposite: in these cover illustrations for the Penguin series Great Loves, David Pearson and Victoria Sawdon have selected images that have a common theme and reflect the content.

Identifying Effective Images

The first step to finding images is to read, or revisit, your brief and identify clearly what you are trying to communicate. This may seem obvious, but it is easy to get involved in the process of designing, and be sidetracked into looking for something that complements the layout, rather than identifying an image that communicates effectively. If the subject matter you are dealing with is lighthearted, it would be logical to select imagery that reflected this both in content and in feel.

The images have been carefully selected to reflect the serious problems highlighted in this web site for Amnesty International.

For this moodboard the designer incorporated texture and rich colours in response to a brief for a package design that conveyed a sense of luxury combined with wholesomeness.

In many cases you will have no choice as to the images to be incorporated into the design but, when you do have a choice it is probably a good idea to start finding the images before you begin your composition. To do this, you need to experiment with ideas in order to identify the sort of image you are looking for. Your starting point may be defined by the brief suggesting a particular type of image. An example of this is a brochure about a specific building, where the sort of image to be included is clear. ❶

On the other hand, the brief or project may be more open-ended, which would enable you to examine a range of possibilities. In this instance, you could explore images that have been formed by different methods such as illustration, mixed media and photographs. Even if the design is web-based, you can incorporate images that use different media providing they can be photographed or scanned effectively. Variety in texture is worth consideration as it can provide visual excitement even if it cannot be touched or felt. The same applies to the use of colour and it is a good idea, if you are given the choice, to investigate the differences between images in full colour and those in black-and-white as well as all the variations in between.

A moodboard is useful for investigating the sort of images to use in a design. It can incorporate a range of materials, not necessarily all image-based – think of a mixture of textures and colours, such as buttons, pens and objects from nature that help you understand the feel you wish to communicate. The items and images you identify through this exercise may not be the ones you use in your design, but they act as prompts. A moodboard is also useful in communicating your ideas to clients or tutors, as well as providing future reference material.

Other considerations may be whether you need to use tactics such as shock or repetition (discussed in later chapters) to communicate with, and attract, your audience. You may also need to think about the format of the images: whether there are any constraints within the design on, for example, long and thin, short and fat or irregular shapes.

Finding the images can be a bit like going shopping and may depend on the sort of person you are. If you are organized, you will have a shopping list and be clear about what you are looking for. This approach has its advantages and is probably quick, but can eliminate the serendipitous quality of the other method, which is random browsing where you pick up images from a variety of sources, often whilst not particularly looking for them, such as when browsing through magazines or the Internet. Whichever method is yours, make sure you select and put into your 'shopping trolley' all the ingredients you need in order to communicate your ideas, in the same way that you would select the ingredients for a cake.

1 Martin Woodtli's design was developed around a specific theme of buildings, which determined the images to be used from the outset.

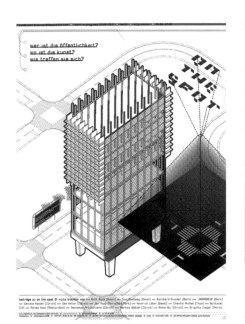

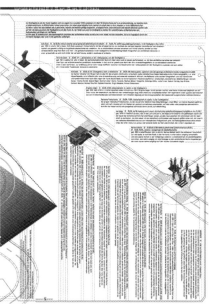

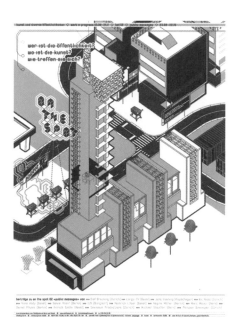

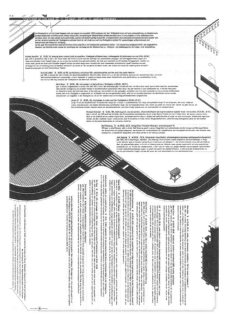

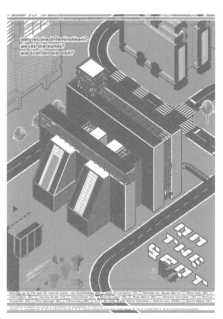

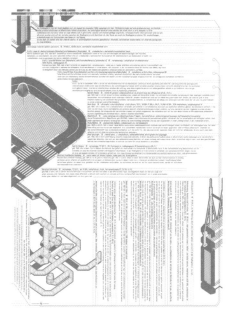

Activity

Choose two existing designs with contrasting messages/mood/feel. These could be posters, magazine spreads or web pages. Using a variety of materials, such as pictures from magazines, swatches of colour or fabric, objects and so on, try to create a moodboard for each design.

Opposite: this design by Grandpeople, has something of the feel of a moodboard with its collection of objects, colours, patterns and shapes.

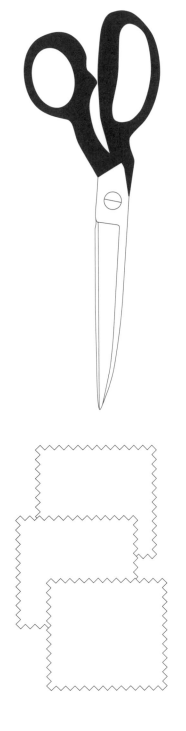

This design by Martin Woodtli conveys the mood of a festival which is reinforced by the hand-produced style of imagery and type used.

COLLECTING FLOWERS

COLLECTING FLOWERS
OSLO ARKITEKTFORENING 100 ÅR
Høst 2006

21.09 ET UTVALG
DIPLOMPROSJEKTER FRA AHO
Kristin, Bernt- og Wenche, Andreassen,
Siri Brudvik, Vegard Ramstad og Kristian
Ribe, Siri Liset, Børge Opheim.
kl.20.00, OAF

11.10 BIG-BJARKE INGELS (DK)
kl.18:00, DogA-Norsk Design- og
Arkitektursenter, Hausmanns gate 16
(NB: Merk sted) OAF i samarbeid med
Norsk Form.
www.big.dk

19.10 ZAHA HADID (GB)
kl.18:00, Arkitektur- og designhøgskolen
i Oslo, Maridalsveien 29.
I forbindelse med OAF's 100 års
markering. OAF i samarbeid med Norsk
Form og AHO.
www.zaha-hadid.com

26.10 S333 (NL)
kl. 20.00, OAF
OAF i samarbeid med Den Nederlandske
Ambassaden.
www.s333.org

5.-22.10 MARKERING AV
OAF'S 100 ÅRS JUBILEUM
Se eget program

OAF 100
OSLO ARKITEKTFORENING

Takk til våre samarbeidspartnere.

09.11 GENERALFORSAMLING
kl. 18.30, OAF
VALERIO OLGIATI (CH)
kl. 20.00, OAF

23.11 ATELIER BOW-WOW (J)
kl. 20.00, OAF
www.bow-wow.jp

30.11 HELENA NJIRIC (HR)
kl. 20.00, OAF

15.12 JULENACHSPIEL, OAF.
Følg med på www.arkitektur.no/oaf

Oslo Arkitektforening
Josefines gate 34, 0351 Oslo
tlf 23 33 24 90 / fax 23 33 24 91
www.arkitektur.no/oaf

www.arkitektur.no/oaf

❶ John Clementson created this design using a combination of two- and three-dimensional items which had to be photographed carefully to produce the raised quality of the finished work.

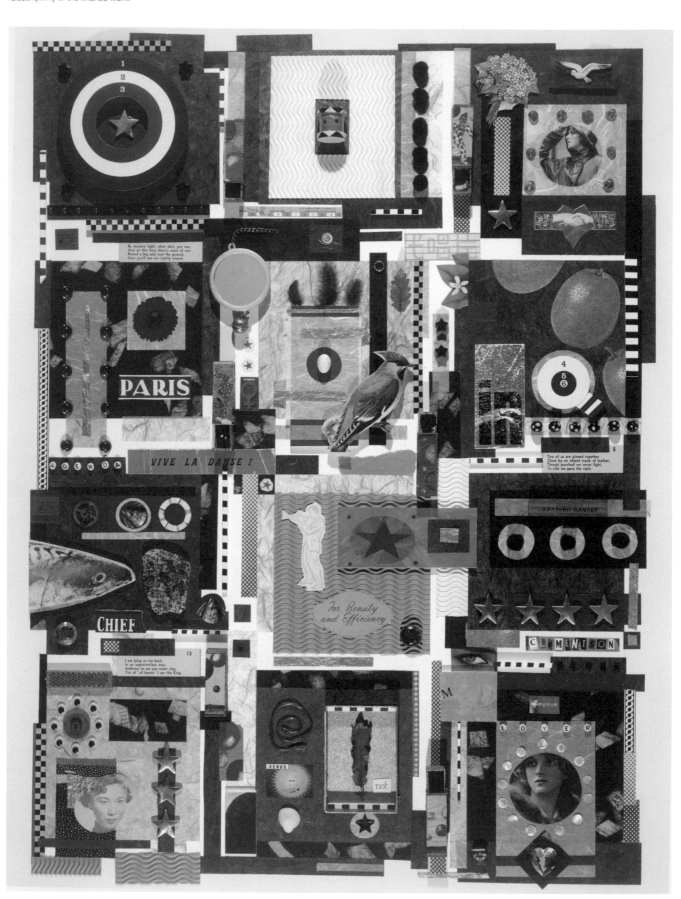

Media Used for Image Production

There are various methods available to produce images, in addition to the obvious ones such as photography and line drawing. In terms of different media, the sky is the limit as long as the medium can be satisfactorily captured in the appropriate format. ❶

 Remember that extra costs and time may be incurred when commissioning a good-quality photograph if an image is in a three-dimensional format, such as a bas-relief, or is of a large scale that will not lend itself to digitizing. Such photography may need to be done on location or require specialist equipment.

Some examples of different media that could be investigated are painting, collage, photomontage, woodcut, linocut, etching, lithograph, screen print and multimedia (physical and digital). Many of these techniques can be reproduced digitally with the right software and may be a cheaper alternative to commissioning a hand-carved linocut, for example.

The eyes in this photomontage seem to be staring at the viewer, making for a strong but somewhat disturbing image.

Appropriate Imagery

In these two posters by Bunch Design the straightforward, easily understood layout on the left contrasts with that of the more complex, detailed information on the right, which does not immediately convey what the poster is about.

Whichever medium, or combination of media, you choose the imagery needs to be appropriate for the audience you wish to reach as well as for the message you are communicating. A good example would be a brochure on products for pensioners. Without stereotyping too much, it is likely that people in this older age range are more likely to require help with seeing small items and therefore you would need to ensure that any imagery in the brochure was clearly legible. You might wish to think twice about using an image that incorporated important fine detail that would be difficult to see easily. This would be particularly important if the image contained text or another element essential to understanding it.

Sourcing Images

Having made some decisions about the images to be used, or having had them decided for you, the next step is to source the images. If you are working with a magazine or large agency, this will often be done for you by picture researchers, art directors, picture editors or art buyers but it is useful, even then, to understand the issues involved.

Although there are many different ways and places for sourcing images, they can be split into two broad types: existing images and commissioned images.

Existing images

There are two forms of existing imagery available for use: free, out-of-copyright material and existing 'available for licence' material which you have to pay for.

Web sites are one of the most frequently used sources of existing images and can fall into either of the above categories in that some are free and some involve fees. You can use existing search engines to try to source images but this is slow and not necessarily productive, and would require you to check ownership. A faster and more efficient method is to use specialist online photograph or illustration stock libraries, of which there are many. Of course, there are readily available images from 'clip art' libraries, which are often free or accompany software packages, but these need to be treated with caution – we've all seen examples of clip art being used to detrimental effect both in print and on the web.

It's a good idea to check any stock images to be certain there is nothing in the background that you don't want included. Sometimes this can be missed if you only see the image on screen or at low resolution.

Stock images are usually available to any subscriber and therefore can often be reproduced several times, which may influence your decision to use them. However, usage fees are generally significantly less than the fees involved in commissioning a bespoke image.

Another source of existing imagery is out-of-copyright photographs and paraphernalia, which designers often source through second-hand markets, car-boot sales or in their attics. This type of image is particularly useful for manipulation and editing, and can be used as found. If you like using this sort of imagery it is worth collecting a stock for future use, although it's advisable to have some sort of cataloguing system for ease of access. The stock may include your own photographs or illustrations, or even those produced by friends and family (with permission of course).

Commissioning imagery

Before you approach any supplier, you need to write a clear brief that identifies exactly what you are looking for. It is also worth, if possible, talking the brief through with whoever you are commissioning, to give them the opportunity to interrogate your ideas and to reassure yourself that they understand what you want. It cannot be stressed enough that you need to be certain about deadlines, fees, licence for use and responsibilities – mistakes cost money and could lose you a job. Sometimes, particularly when you have worked regularly with a creative supplier, you may feel confident in giving them minimal guidelines or, once they know your working style, feel you can trust them to come up with a range of ideas.

Basically, there are two kinds of creative supplier – illustrators and photographers – and there are a few differences in the way you communicate with them. Probably the main difference is the input you might expect to have during the developmental process. When commissioning an illustration you would expect to see a rough idea to 'sign off' prior to completion of the final artwork. You would expect to be able to add or ask for changes at this stage. However, you will usually receive only one final image to use. In commissioning photography you would expect to see a selection of images to choose from, with major or minimal differences between them, and could often be present at the final 'shoot' in order to make sure you get what you want.

Places to look for illustrators and photographers include: agencies who hold portfolios of the creatives they represent and who take a percentage of the fee paid; professional organizations such as the Association of Illustrators (in the UK); industry publications, which often host advertisements for freelancers as well as showcasing new work; and degree shows and other exhibitions of student and graduate work. There are also lots of web sites where you can access freelancers' portfolios.

However you source your images, it is essential that you ensure their quality, as we have had to do for this book, and that they are suitable for your chosen method of production.

Image quality and suitability

It is not usually the production person's role, be they a printer or web designer, to ensure that images are of the correct standard, but they may advise you if they are not.

Image size is discussed in more depth in Chapter 7 but, for now, it is worth remembering that images used in print usually need to be high resolution, 300 dpi at 100 percent size, whereas those to be used on screen normally need to be only 72 dpi. In terms of quality, if you look at images reproduced in newspapers you will see that they are not particularly good as the images are usually medium resolution, 100 to 150 dpi, whereas in books and magazines the quality is better. This is because the resolution of the image relates to the printing process which, for newspapers, is cheap and very fast on low-quality stock. ❶

Often, in low-quality print, a selection of imagery that has strong contrast and shape, such as line drawings, can give a crisper and stronger look than a photograph, for which it is difficult to reproduce the full tonal range. High-quality print, on the other hand, such as that used for art books, reproduces tones well and allows the full range of images available in different media to be explored.

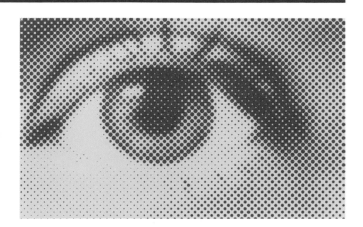

❶ These examples demonstrate the difference between a low resolution image (top) and one with high resolution (bottom).

The Audience

As discussed earlier in this chapter, recognizing your audience is an important aspect of image selection. Differences in age, gender and social background, for example, need to be taken into account where necessary. However, sometimes a design may need to span a wide range of people and even nationalities, in which case it is important not to disengage any particular section of the population by, for instance, inadvertently ignoring, annoying or patronizing them. This also relates to variations in cultural interpretation, such as the symbolism associated with some colours, as discussed in Chapter 5.

Understanding your audience is not always straightforward. Not only do you sometimes have to consider a large section of the population; there are also times when you need to consider a hidden audience. This is often the case with children's products, such as picture books, where it is the parent or another adult who is the purchaser, and a participant in its use – usually by reading the book to the child. There is a dilemma here: do you design for the adult or the child or try to design for both?

 Graphic designers, art directors and other creatives often make the mistake of designing for themselves. This is similar to buying a present for someone based on what you like rather than what they would want.

Meanings of Images

If you saw this sign, what would it mean to you? Would it mean your dog was allowed to foul the area or not allowed to foul the area? Or would you see it as a warning that dogs had fouled the area? The meaning was not clear, although it was interpreted as being an area where dogs were allowed to foul.

To return to variations in cultural interpretations, it is always worth thinking about the signs and symbols you use and whether your audience will understand or misunderstand them. In the example shown above, the image could be interpreted in various ways and is not at all straightforward. It could be seen as being humorous as the symbol for the dog has a cartoonish appearance.

Humour is often seen as a good way of attracting an audience but, as with most gimmicks, it is a double-edged sword, as it is down to personal taste and is subject, yet again, to individual interpretation. Humour does not necessarily cross continents or borders. As you have probably gathered, there are lots of considerations in relation to audiences, and these are covered in more detail in Chapter 4, as is a more in-depth look at meanings.

Social Responsibility

SMOKING CAUSES FATAL DISEASES

Chief Medical   Officers' Warning
5mg Tar   0.5mg Nicotine

This advertisement for cigarettes uses obesity, which could be considered offensive by some, to convey its rather obscure message about the brand 'Silk Cut'.

Designers are subject to continually changing social, ethical and legal boundaries which, with the increasing globalization of visual communication, continue to be in a constant state of flux. The power of the image relies on the audience reacting in some way; and this is relevant to the use of stereotypes to convey messages such as those relating to race, disability, gender, sexual orientation, religious belief and age.

When using images for such messages, there are 'lines', albeit somewhat indistinct, that should not be crossed. Where these lines are drawn differs from culture to culture and is not, particularly when dealing with religion, contained by physical borders. For example, to a secular readership the publication

of a cartoon of Muhammad in a Danish newspaper in 2005 may seem a harmless, satirical, visual trick, but it was deeply offensive to many practising Muslims. The fact that it was published in one country is irrelevant as its publication, and how this was interpreted, had an effect throughout the world.

As well as social responsibilities, there may be a range of personal/political/ethical lines that you wish to draw and apply to your work: this is, of course, your individual choice. Additionally, designers have a moral and legal responsibility to work within the ethical and legal guidelines applicable to the country or countries where their work is published.

Legal Responsibilities: Copyright

The following are very broad guidelines and reflect current regulations in the United Kingdom and the United States. You are advised to check the legal situation in the country or countries of publication, and also any variations applicable to certain sorts of images. It is best to clear up any copyright issues early on so that you are free to get on with designing – it also ensures that they won't compromise any deadlines.

'Copyright' means exactly what it says. It is the right to copy something, whether this is physical, like a photocopy or print, or digital, as in a file from a digital camera or scanned image. Normally, when an image is produced the copyright remains with the author of the work. Copyright exists for 70 years after the originator's death, although there may be situations where it is held by institutions or owners of the work, such as galleries. In these cases permission needs to be obtained from the institution before use. It is important to note that ownership of the artwork does not necessarily equate with ownership of the copyright. For instance, if a person sells a painting to someone, the copyright remains with the artist, not the new owner. Therefore, if you wished to use the painting in your design you would need to arrange a licence with the illustrator, not the owner.

There are, however, exceptions to this rule. In the case of a photographer who is commissioned to take a photograph of something – let's say, a studio shot of a plate of food for a packaging project – the commissioning client would own the copyright, as the photographer is supplying technical expertise rather than creative ideas. If the photographer created a shot of a still life (also a plate of food) as a creative solution to a more open brief, the copyright would belong to the photographer.

Be aware that images are not always what they seem: part of an image or something included in an image, such as a brand, will sometimes have its own copyright issues. Even though you may have obtained an image from a legitimate source, if a trademark, a famous person or other owned item or identity is part of it you may need to obtain permission to use it. A possible alternative is to edit out the problem; this is discussed further in Chapter 6.

If you are commissioned as a designer, the copyright in your designs is owned by the client. Similarly, if you produce images as a full-time employee, your employer owns the copyright.

Before you get out your digital scissors and start cropping and chopping an image, use caution: there is something called a 'right to integrity' which means you cannot change someone's work if it might damage their reputation. This applies to any manipulation of an image and also to the way in which an image is used. ❶

Remember the golden rule: do not do unto others that which you would not have others do unto you. Using images without permission is unfair to the originator of the image, and also to those who do follow copyright regulations.

 You need to think carefully about taking sections of images for use in composites such as photomontages or collages. Make sure the resulting image is unique, and not just a replica of the original sections with some minor adjustments.

When commissioning an image, it is unlikely that you will require its full copyright. Normally, you will only require the right to use it for a specific purpose and for a specific period of time. In this case, you would purchase a licence that specifies the exact use of the image. For example, you may require it for a book cover, for a timeframe of 10 years, to be published in a specific country or countries. The cost of the licence usually relates to these three factors. This is why the fees paid in advertising, where an image may be used many times in a campaign, are higher than they are in editorial design, where the image is used once for one issue of a magazine or one edition of a book.

 Do not assume that because an image is on a web site it is available for use without a fee or copyright permission. Always check with the owner or originator of the image.

Picture credits

When you use an image in editorial matter, be sure to credit the work to the originator. Credits are usually included near the image – in newspapers and magazines they often run vertically alongside the image, in small type. You may wish to make more of the creator of an image if it helps to attract your audience – an example of this approach is the publicity given to Mario Testino's photographs for Benetton's advertising campaigns. Credits in books are often included as a separate list, either at the front of the book or at the back. For further reference, an appendix at the back of this book includes publications and institutions that can be contacted for information on copyright and licensing.

❶ Cropping this illustration by Inksurge caused it to lose its overall effect and changed the image's meaning. (We sought permission to show this image cropped.)

Case Study
Logo: 5th Berlin Biennial for Contemporary Art, Ludovic Balland

1.

These three images show the original archive image, the original letterform, Jury-regular (designed by Balland), and the way in which the image is combined with the letterform. Changing the image to black and white rather than colour reinforces the historical feel.

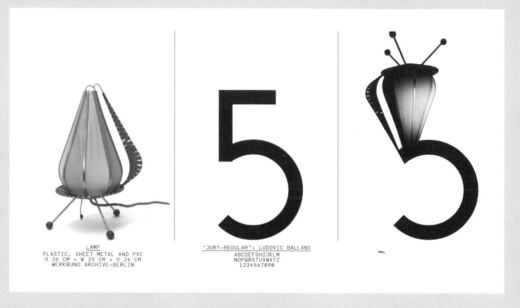

LAMP
PLASTIC, SHEET METAL AND PVC
H 36 CM × W 25 CM × D 24 CM
WERKBUND ARCHIVE-BERLIN

"JURY-REGULAR": LUDOVIC BALLAND
ABCDEFGHIJKLM
NOPQRSTUVWXYZ
1234567890

2.

The designer wanted to incorporate images of Berlin in the final logo, to relate the design to the city's cultural history and underpin his retro theme. After initial desktop research, he realized that the easiest way to get the architectural images he needed was to take his own photographs as the buildings and sites were easily accessible.

This approach ensured that there was no need to obtain copyright permission for existing images. It is worth noting that Balland had access to a good-quality camera, which enabled him to produce images of a suitable quality, size and format. Also, his design education meant he had experience of composition and photographic techniques.

One of Balland's colour photographs, the letterform, and the composite formed from these, are shown in these images. In all the designs in the series the buildings in the pictures are isolated from their backgrounds to give them identifiable shapes that work with the letter B. Balland seems to be treating the letterforms as architectural shapes, which resonates with the biennial's theme of memories of the city.

HOTEL RITZ-CARLTON
POTSDAMER PLATZ, BERLIN MITTE
SOURCE: INTERNET
11.04.2006

"JURY-REGULAR": LUDOVIC BALLAND
ABCDEFGHIJKLM
NOPQRSTUVWXYZ
1234567890

Ludovic Balland's brief was to design a series of illustrated letter Bs and number 5s to form the B5 logo for the 5th Berlin Biennial for Contemporary Art. The title of the biennial was 'When Things Cast No Shadows', which related to the overall theme: the collective memory of the city. The designer wanted to incorporate images with the letterforms in order to give them a more visual presence, suitable for an art-based exhibition.

After initial research, Balland identified the kinds of image he was looking for. He was keen to use ones that were directly associated with Berlin and, if possible, had a historical context. Researching these was a broad-based and quick way to find a lot of information. However, further in-depth research was

needed to find specific images of a sufficiently high resolution and size to be used in print-based work. Balland tried a variety of sources and finally settled on one that could provide suitable images in the right format: the Werkbund Archive in Berlin.

Considered to be one of the precursors of the Bauhaus movement, the Werkbund was founded in 1907 and the archive holds examples of design from this time. Balland considered these artefacts to be suitable for his project as they are from the past and so relate to the title of the biennial.

3.

These two finished pieces combine Balland's range of B5 designs with the supporting typeface and other texts used for the biennial's promotional material. The B5s have become abstracted and seem to be neither type nor image, but a hybrid of the two – which was the designer's intention.

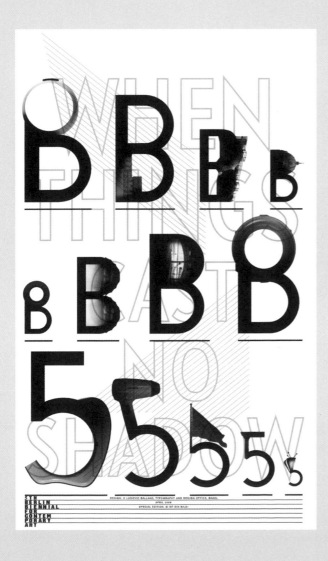

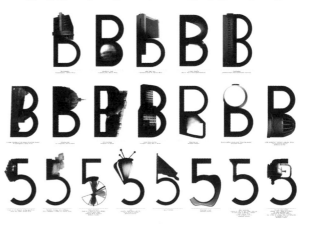

MAP
You are here: Journeys in Contemporary Art

PAULINA OLOWSKA / SCOTT MYLES /
HENRIK OLESEN / LORIS GRÉAUD /
ROB KENNEDY / ANN BOWMAN /
GLASGOW / NEW YORK / LONDON

Issue 14
Summer 2008
£4.95

MAP
You are here: Journeys in Contemporary Art

DUNCAN CAMPBELL / JG BALLARD /
JORDAN WOLFSON / DOT DOT DOT /
ANDREAS DOBLER / ALAN STANNERS /
TORONTO / TRENTINO / BELFAST

Issue 15
Autumn 2008
£4.95

Francis McKee traces the path
of Belgian artist Francis Alÿs as he
explores the boundaries between
politics, poetry and art

'Once there was a man who …
pushed a block of ice across
a vast city until it melted and
disappeared; an artist who
sent a peacock to take his place
in an important gathering
of his peers; a man who
persuaded a small army of
workers to move an immense
sand dune armed only with
shovels; a solitary walker who
one day emerged from a shop
holding a loaded pistol…'

MOTHER SCULPTURE

Karla Black is a young Glasgow
sculptor, with a thing of
once fragile and yet temporal.
Its materials slowly belie making
structure the chaotic

Melissa Jeffries travels to Monterrey
and discovers bright lights of Scotland
and asphalt, a major showing of 13
British artists in Mexico

Matteo Cuiros talks to 5th Berlin
Biennial (sbb) curators Elena
Filipovic and Adam Szymczyk
about the city, the biennial
concept and the philosophies
to edun around this edition

Structure and Layout

There are general rules that can be applied to most layouts but, as most people have found at some time or other, rules are there to be broken. However, the basic guidelines for layout provide a good basis from which to develop creative ideas for communication – and an underpinning structure helps to give a design cohesion.

When a picture is framed there is often a larger space at the bottom of the mount than at the top. This conveys a balanced feel so the picture or image does not look as if it is about to drop off. This principle has traditionally been used as a guideline for margin construction to ensure pleasing proportions in the structure of a page.

There are certain factors that should, normally, be taken into consideration when a basic layout is designed, such as space, format, amount of text, number of images, the time and cost involved and the purpose of the design. Other issues that may influence the design are whether you are limited in terms of typefaces, colours, size of images or the way the images are used. It is easy to see these factors as limitations but it is more constructive to use them as the starting point or basis from which to develop ideas.

Opposite: these designs by Studio 8 for MAP magazine have a lively, interesting feel produced using a strong underlying structure.

Collecting
the Elements

This double-page spread contains many elements: image, text, title, subhead, captions, icon, credit line and the equivalent of a header/footer surrounding the page number on the right-hand page.

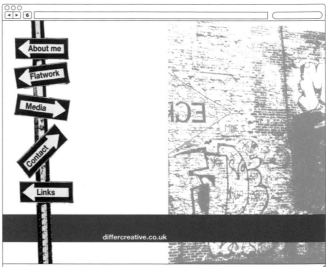

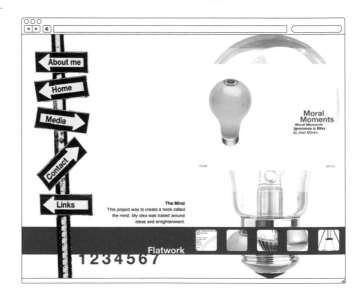

Before the structure of a layout is designed, it's necessary to determine what the various elements within it will be, and in order to do this it is useful to know some terminology. The following is a basic list:

Image: This could be a photograph or illustration, or a picture produced by other means.

Text: Words that make up the story, article or main message; also called body copy, copy or type.

Title: Also called heading, headline or head.

Subhead: Secondary heading to the title.

Caption: Text that explains an image.

Icon: Pictogram used as a link or metaphor to replace text.

Credit lines: The names of the originators of works used in a design.

Header/footer: Small section of text at the top or base of a page; often the publication's name and date of issue or, in books, could be the name of the book and/or the chapter.

Josh Gidman has used various elements in designing his web pages. He incorporates icons (boxes within the red block at the bottom of the page), links (arrows on the signpost on the left of each page), images and text on all pages.

Activity
*Cut up existing layouts and experiment with rearranging them,
adding or subtracting items if necessary.*

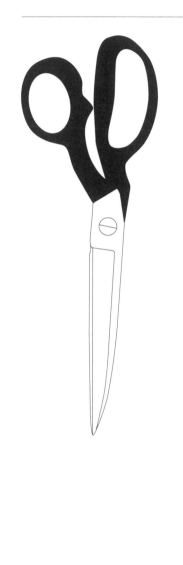

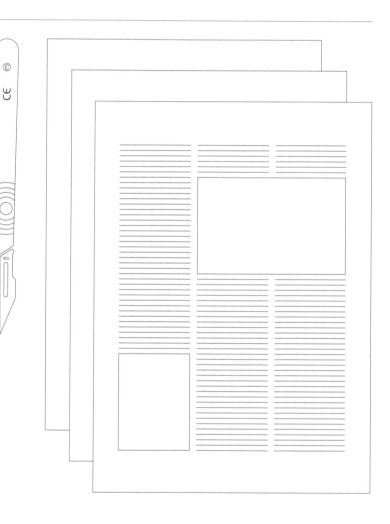

Before You Start

At the outset of any design, you need to ensure that you understand the subject matter, and set aside time to search for ideas, information and inspiration from a variety of sources. If you are designing a poster, for example, don't just look at other posters for ideas. Look at a variety of ways of communicating visually, such as web pages or information graphics. Look at other sorts of communication such as films, books or paintings. Investigate aspects of design, such as shop windows, landscape design and architecture, that are not normally associated with this sort of work. Also, start experimenting with different ideas before worrying too much about the structure.

 Try not to invest too much time and effort in any one layout/idea at the beginning – put ideas down roughly and quickly; you can sort through them later. Think quantity (not quality). Avoid the temptation to stick with your first idea just to save time and money.

Thumbnails

Thumbnails, or small sketches of different layout ideas, are a good way of getting all your ideas down quickly (like brainstorming) so that you can pick and choose easily, or combine different ideas before working them up to full size. This is also an opportunity to experiment with different formats, if that is possible, for the job in hand.

These thumbnails show how Jenny Tune develops ideas for a book cover design. She experiments with different combinations of text and image, indicating the image with a box with diagonal lines crossing between opposite corners.

 Never rely on a thumbnail for knowing what the finished piece will look like. Many things work well at one size but not if they are scaled up or down.

Top: a storyboard showing John Clementson's development of the illustrations for each section of the narrative of *The Crow and the Hawk*.

Bottom: A finished spread from *The Crow and the Hawk*.

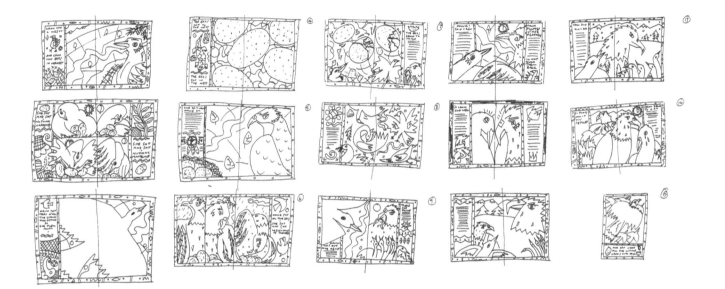

Another use of thumbnails is in editorial design, where a flat plan helps the designer and editor to formulate the structure of the publication. A storyboard or dummy book is another way of helping a designer to formulate sequence, narrative and visual rhythm, and is essential when structuring pictorial content such as in a children's picture book or graphic novel.

A flat plan is used to ensure that all the components are present and in the right place, and also helps the designer to work out how to arrange them and have an overview of the entire work. A storyboard is used to provide a sense of the narrative; for an illustrated book, the illustrations would tell the story. Storyboards are often used for animation sequences and short films and videos, including advertisements.

The designer has sketched out a rough plan of where images and text fit into an exhibition catalogue.

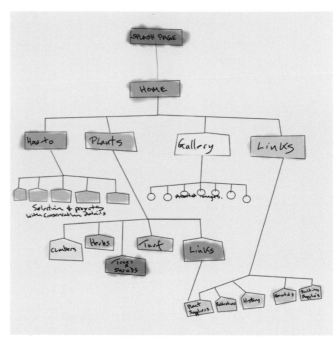

Carol Cooper's flow chart for a web site shows how she is working out the links and connections between the various pages.

An overview of the completed work is also necessary when designing a web site. The structure of the entire site, in the form of a flow chart or site map, as well as individual pages, should be considered in order to ensure that there is continuity and flow and that the site has cohesion.

 When designing a grid for editorial matter it is worth remembering that the print on the reverse of the page sometimes shows through and could interfere visually with your design.

Structure Related to Content

Essential to the structure of a design is a good understanding of the content. It is, therefore, important to read any copy provided carefully, and discuss its subject with the client or, if you are at college, your tutor. Always ask questions in order to clarify any areas or aspects that are unclear.

All the elements – for example, images, titles, copy and space – within a layout must work together to convey the message that the content represents: what the magazine, web site or package is about.

Different types of content require different layouts; active layouts would be used to reflect dynamic content whereas a passive layout would be more appropriate for serious content. An article about salsa dancing would probably require an active layout that conveys the rhythm and feeling of the dance. On the other hand, an article about finance may require a passive layout that would underpin a more serious message.

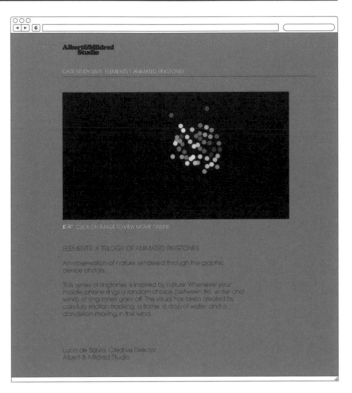

This design by Luca de Salvia links to a ringtone on a mobile phone screen and has plenty of movement, conveying a feeling of interest and excitement.

Web structure can be much more fluid than print, as images and other graphic elements can move around. So, if the content is serious, perhaps there should be less movement, in the same way that a passive layout suggests serious content in printed matter.

When thinking about structure, it is very easy to get carried away juxtaposing the images and text and lose sight of the purpose of the communication or the message. There are many layouts that are inappropriate to their content. For example, an A4, five-column grid with lots of images of varying sizes would not normally be used to communicate a gloomy message.

This design by Ludovic Balland employs a variety of overlapping images combined with small sections of text, some used at right angles to each other. This provides an active layout appropriate for a promotional poster for a cinema.

Activity
*Choose a magazine page and put a piece of tracing paper
over it. Then try to draw the underlying grid, identifying how
many columns of text there are and how the images, margins or
captions are positioned.*

The Carnival of Sean web site has lots of
activity and movement. The content and
the way it is portrayed are appropriate to
the web site's name.

This web site has a fairly serious content
and therefore the layout is quite passive
and calm with a well-defined structure.

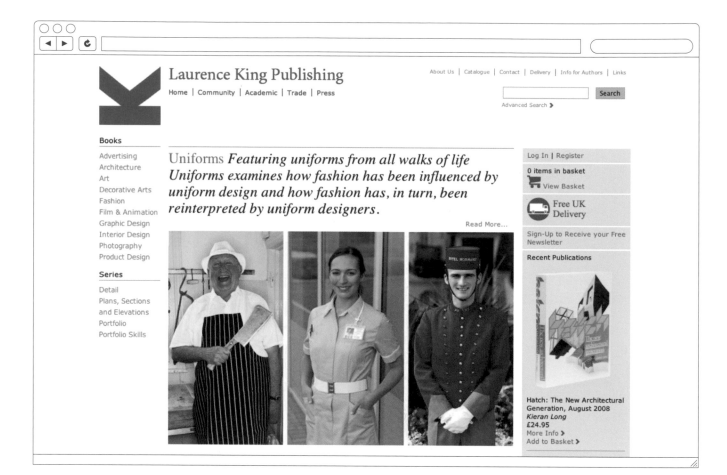

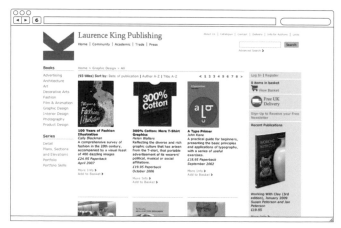

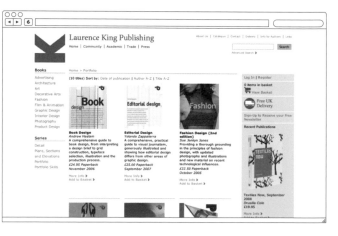

The balance of image to text may also inform the approach to a layout. Text-heavy content, for example, could denote a serious subject, and could also involve practical considerations as incorporating all the necessary information allows less room for manoeuvre. However, much communication relies on a headline or image to attract the reader in the first place, leaving information such as that required by law to the small print which is often at the end of a document or on the back of a package.

An example of this type of communication is packaging, where the product's identity has to be on the part that faces the consumer when it is stacked or displayed. Also, as you are telling a story in a tight space, the structure or layout needs to reflect the message clearly: what is the customer buying? ❶

On the other hand, when there is very little content in the form of text and images the challenge is to fill the available space. In this situation, a small amount of information in a large space, with lots of space around the elements of the layout, often evokes affluence.

A combination of these two scenarios is probably the most difficult trick to pull off. An example is an introductory web page that has to indicate content of a serious nature, which may be text-heavy, but also has to indicate something interesting and therefore needs to be eye-catching. ❷

In some circumstances there is no formalized structure, and the design develops from a starting point, such as an image or a title within the confines of the page format. However, a structure often helps to communicate information in much the same way that an essay needs a beginning, middle and end to get its message across.

Finally, it is important to make sure the images you place in a design relate consistently to the text they are intended to illustrate. If you move or change images remember to check the adjacent copy for consistency.

 A common pitfall in many magazines is the dislocation between the image and the relevant text. This has been exacerbated by the ability of modern desktop publishing software to link text boxes throughout a document. So always read the copy and check that the images selected for your design are still relevant to the text adjacent to them.

An effective method for providing an underpinning structure is the use of a grid – most commonly used in editorial design for magazines, newspapers and books.

❶ This supermarket display demonstrates the necessity for the customer-facing part of a product's packaging to convey its content clearly and attract the consumer, especially when displayed alongside other products.

❷ Parc&Maul's design uses an unusual image to lure the viewer into their web site, which has quite a few text-heavy pages. These are necessary in order to describe the project and their progress on it as well as including a blog.

60 years } Human Rights

no if's, no but's
every human deserves rights

Unity over Division
Hope over Despair
Solidarity over Self-
interest

1|2 the worlds population has one
or more of their human rights
violated on a daily basis...

**Galvanize Political Will And
Make Human Rights a Reality
--Not Just A Paper Promise--**

Opposite: the intuitive poster design, shown opposite, by Katrin Schweigert does not have an underpinning structure or grid. The designer has placed the text around a strong image.

Top: this book cover design by Astrid Stavro has a very formal structure which makes the publication easily identifiable and gives it a formal and organized appearance.

Bottom: Marijke Cobbenhagen's design uses juxtaposition of images in a variety of sizes and formats to create a lively layout whilst keeping a fairly formal structure.

❶ In the design shown opposite, Grandpeople have used images outside and across the grid structure.

Grids

In the same way that you cannot see a skeleton when you look at a person, the grid is the invisible structure underneath a design. You need to visualize this structure clearly to ensure that your design has cohesion and communicates effectively. The grid or format will determine where all the different elements, such as text and images, go; but, at the same time, it needs to allow for flexibility and diversity.

The format, whether it is an A2 poster or A5 folded brochure, makes a difference to the way in which the grid is structured. Most designers work to standard-sized formats because these are cheaper to produce than non-standard ones.

The starting point for many editorial grids is the type and how it reads in columns. This, combined with margin measurements, defines the look and feel of the page. Other forms of design, such as posters and web pages, have much less text and therefore often have an underpinning structure but not necessarily a grid.

Although an underpinning grid is needed to give cohesion to editorial design, you may use images outside the grid structure or across it, as well as within the columns. Unless you want your design to look very structured and formal, it is best to use the grid as a guide rather than as a straitjacket. ❶

This applies to the horizontal aspect of the grid as well as to the vertical one dictated by columns. When designing a grid, keep in mind horizontal flow as this will help to guide the reader around the page. It can also help with continuity and consistency, but needs to be carefully considered in order to avoid too rigid a structure that inhibits creativity and variety.

As stated earlier, it is best to experiment with thumbnail designs before transferring the best of them to a computer for working up. It is always worth experimenting with more than one grid/format and you may find that a combination of ideas works best. This may also help to maintain a reader's interest as, quite often, a similar grid used throughout a magazine can make it look all the same and rather boring.

A good grid is a guide and ordinarily does not print (heard but not seen). It is essential to give structure and continuity to a publication, but it is important to ensure that the structure is appropriate for the content and the viewer or reader.

Appropriate grids

In a similar way that a grid or structure is used to reflect content – a structure that suggests serious content would not be used to convey short pieces of light information – it should also be appropriate for the audience or reader. For example, if an audience is young and requires short pieces of information, a web page or poster designed for them would probably use more illustration than text to keep them engaged, and a multicolumn grid would provide the flexibility to break up the page more than a single- or two-column grid.

There are, however, times when there is no choice about the grid or structure. This is often the case in editorial design.

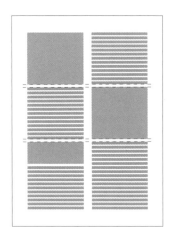
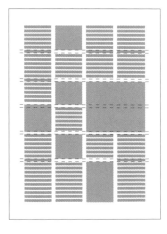

These two diagrams illustrate the vertical and horizontal structure of simple grids. The first diagram shows a two-column grid and the second diagram demonstrates the increased flexibility for placing and arranging text and images that a four-column grid allows.

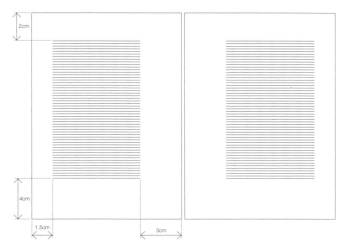

This diagram shows the classical proportions on a left-hand book page. The right-hand page is a mirror image. The inside margin is usually wider to take account of the binding which prevents the book being opened flat and therefore makes reading difficult near its spine.

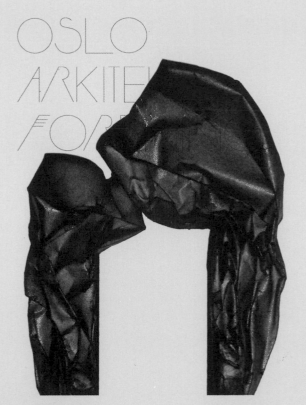

OSLO
ARKITEKT
FOR

2.2
BAUMSCHLAGER
EBERLE ARCHITEKTEN
(Østerrike)
v/Dietmar Eberle
CHRISTIAN AUGUSTS GATE 23 / KL 19:00

I forbindelse med åpningen av utstillingen "Nyskapende østerriksk arkitektur" i Kunsthallen på Tullinløkka.
Baumschlager – Eberle er det største arkitektkontoret i Vorarlberg og har spilt en viktig rolle i utviklingen av innovativ arkitektur i regionen.

www.baumschlagereberle.com

18.2
DAN GRAHAM
(USA)
"OWN WORKS"
AHO, MARIDALSVEIEN 29 / NB! LØRDAG KL 11:00

I forbindelse med OCA seminaret: DRAFT DECEIT (ADDENDUM).
I samarbeid med Arkitekt- og Designhøgskolen i Oslo og Oslo Arkitektforening.

American Artist, 1942. Born in Urbana, IL.
Lives and works in New York.

www.oca.no

9.3
TESTBED STUDIO
(Sverige)
OAF / KL 19:00

Testbed Studio arbeider med analyse, konseptutvikling og design innenfor arkitektur og urbanisme. Gjennom sin AIKIDO metode kombinerer de innovative ideer med pragmatiske løsninger for å utvikle problematiske situasjoner til noe positivt.

www.testbedstudio.com

16.3
VAN BELLE &
MEDINA
(Belgia)
OAF / KL 19:00

Van Belle & Medina er et internasjonalt kontor med base i Antwerpen. Kontoret ble etablert i 2004 etter at arkitektene Kurt Van Belle og Patricia Medina Prieto vant en 1. premie i den internasjonale arkitektkonkurransen Europan 7.

www.vanbellemedina.com

30.3
DORTE MANDRUP
(Danmark)
OAF / KL 19:00

Dorte Mandrup Arkitekter ApS ble etablert i København i 1999 og har i dag ca. 30 ansatte. De arbeider visjonært i krysstfeltet mellom dynamisk og kontemplative rom - mellom tonsilt og nøje.

www.dortemandrup.dk

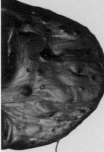

20.4-22.4
OCA CONFERENCE: ISMS
AHO, MARIDALSVEIEN 29
SE ANNONSERING FOR TIDSPUNKT

Konferanse i regi av Marta Kuzma, Office For Contemporary Art. I samarbeid med Arkitekt- og Designhøgskolen i Oslo og Oslo Arkitektforening.

www.oca.no

11.5
CH+QS
(Spania)
CHURTICHAGA - QUADRA-SALCEDO ARQUITECTOS
OAF / KL 19:00

Churtichaga + Quadra Salcedo Arquitectos ble etablert i Madrid i 1995 av Josemaria de Churtichaga og Cayetana de la Quadra-Salcedo.
Kontoret har gjort seg bemerket blant annet med et biblioteket og et kulturssenter utenfor Madrid.

www.chqs.net

1.6
RICK JOY
(USA)
OAF / KL 19:00

"The silence in great music is often more profound than the sounds."

www.rickjoy.com

27.4
GENERALFORSAMLING
OAF / KL 17:00

B-ARCHITECTEN
(Belgia)
OAF / KL 19:00

Evert Crols, Dirk Engelen og Sven Grooten studerte ved The Berlage Instituts i Amsterdam. I 1997 starter de B-architecten i Antwerpen. De arbeider med svært varierte prosjekter, fra boliger til offentlige bygninger, butikkinteriører og scenografi for utstilling og teater.

www.b-architecten.be

9.6
SOMMERFEST
TID OG STED ANNONSERES SENERE. FØLG MED!

COLLEC
TING
F
OWE RR

OSLO
ARKITEKTFORENING 100 ÅR

EN ARKITEKTUR OG
KUNSTANTOLOGI

Våren 2006

Retur: Oslo Arkitektforening
Josefines gate 34
0351 Oslo

Telefon: 23 33 24 90
E-post: oaf@arkitektur.no
www.arkitektur.no/oaf

Satt 2006. Aleksandra Kosberg, Marianne Borge, Julia Vran, Helge Lunder, Hanne Øverland, Sigurd Aanby, Lisbeth Funck / Daglig drift: Sigrun Karin Rodal
Takk til våre samarbeidspartnere:

Martin Woodtli's dynamic design for soDA,
a magazine for visual culture, has an
underpinning multicolumn grid that can be
adapted to a variety of combinations and
page layouts.

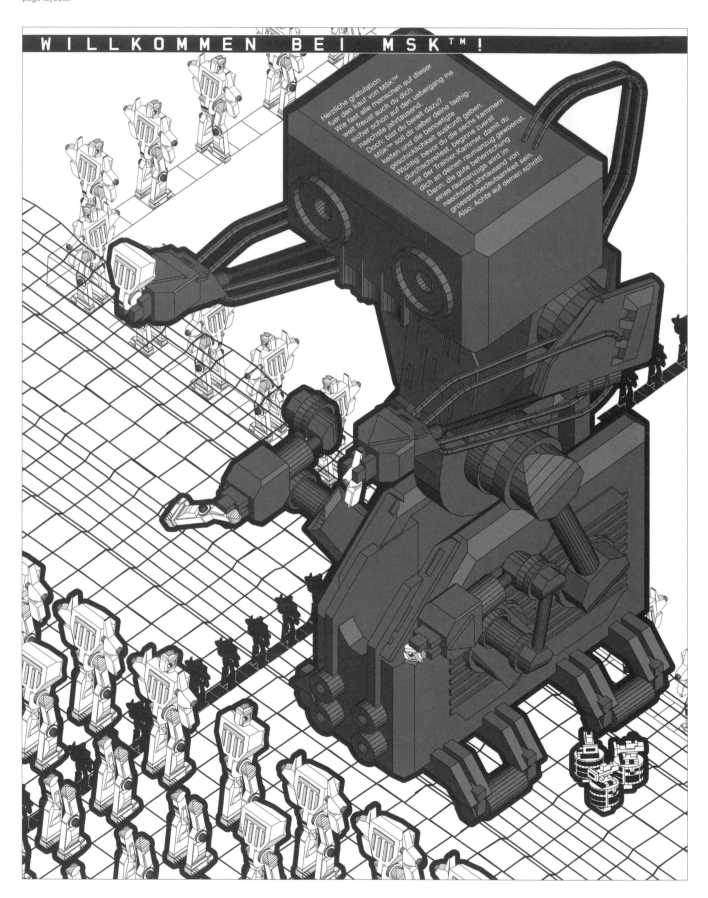

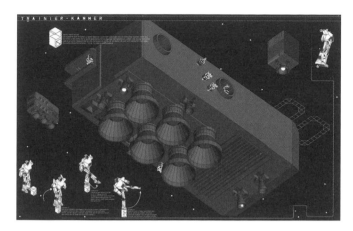

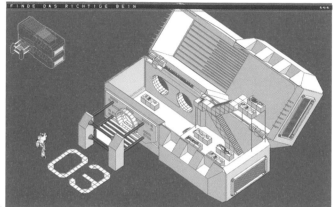

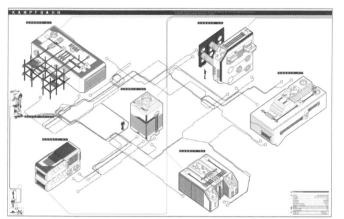

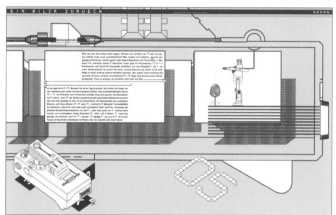

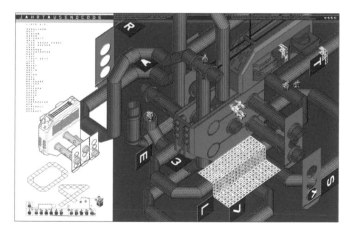

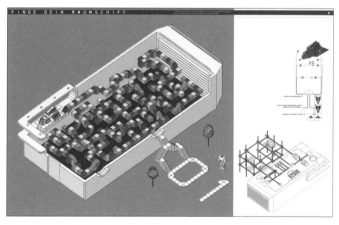

House Styles
and Templates

Many editorial designers work within given house styles or templates. On magazines, for example, they usually work to a house style that gives the publication an overall identity and ensures that readers can tell which publication they are looking at, no matter what page they open it at. These guidelines are not normally totally rigid, and allow some freedom for the designer to interpret content or be adventurous.

Often a publication has a range of different style sheets to reflect the different types of article included; a serious article would have a two-column grid whereas a letters page would use a four-column grid to give maximum flexibility for short pieces of text. Some magazines employ more than one type of grid, allowing the designer to accommodate different kinds of content.

Style sheets can be created with desktop publishing software and many programs include style sheets and templates that can be customized.

In the same way that people who are part of a particular social group wear similar, but not exactly the same, clothes, and are identified by their style, so style sheets, templates, house styles and corporate identity are about belonging and identification. For example, the use of a style sheet for a series of books, such as *The Chronicles of Narnia*, identifies both the individual titles and the series to which they belong. ❶

Designers may also be constrained by working within corporate design guidelines. These are similar to house styles, but may often include strict rules on the type and quality of images, and the way items in a layout are used. ❷

Some elements in a design are inseparable from structure if the overall feel of the design is going to be maintained. These can be simple things, such as ensuring continuity in the use of page numbering and headers, and image and text alignment.

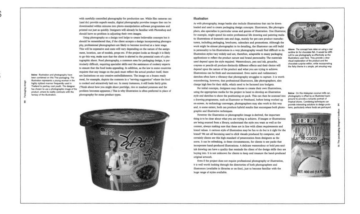

These double-page spreads demonstrate the use of style sheets to maintain cohesion throughout a publication while allowing for variation in appearance to maintain interest.

❶ In Astrid Stavro's design, the books are linked by the layout of their covers and the use of similar images to identify them as belonging to a series.

Zygmunt Bauman
Confianza y temor en la ciudad
Vivir con extranjeros

Ramin Jahanbegloo
Elogio de la diversidad
Prólogo de Juan Goytisolo

Ilana Shmueli
Fragmentos de una época
Una carta
Prólogo de Rob Riemen

Rob Riemen
Nobleza de espíritu
Tres ensayos sobre una idea olvidada
Prólogo de George Steiner

Marc Fumaroli
Educación de la libertad
Prólogo de Juan Goytisolo

Wolf Lepenies
Melancolía y utopía

ARCADIA · ARCADIA · ARCADIA · ARCADIA · ARCADIA · ARCADIA

❷ When designing this series of banknotes, Martin Woodtli had to work within specific guidelines. The exceptional detail is a characteristic of this sort of design, intended to deter forgery.

❶ A page from a catalogue for an
illustration exhibition in which the captions
are aligned to the base of images.

❷ Ed Fella's web site has continuity in the
style of the headings and the icons used
for navigation, as well as the folders used
for images of his work.

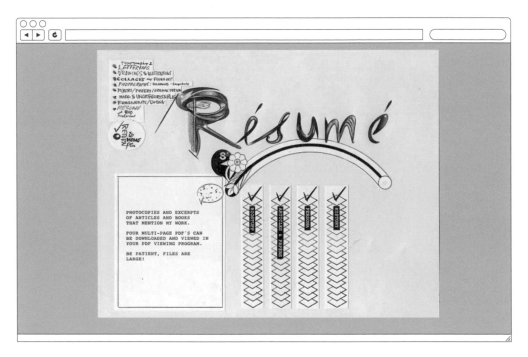

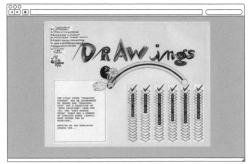

Aligning Images with Text

Consistency in the way images and text are placed on a page in relation to each other can make the page easier to read, helping to guide the eye between different items. For example, for readability it is useful to align the top or the bottom of an image with the top or bottom of lines of text. This is only one way of aligning images with text but, particularly in editorial matter, it is useful to have something that makes a link between the two that is not necessarily apparent to the reader. ❶

There are other ways of communicating the overall feel and cohesion of a design. Examples are the consistent use of graphic elements such as rules (lines), printer's fingers, scissors or a pictogram of a house as a metaphor for the home page on a web site. In the images opposite there is a consistent use of icons on individual pages of the same web site but each page, viewed individually, is easily identifiable as part of the whole. ❷

In editorial matter there are conventions related to cohesion and production.

The graphic device known as a printer's finger, or fist or 'manicule' (amongst other names), was used to mark a paragraph or draw attention to something in early printing. Henry VIII drew pointing fingers in margins of documents to draw attention to an item.

Conventions

Publishers of books, magazines and newspapers have conventions for the work they produce. For example, *Guardian Style* (David Marsh, 2007) includes guidelines on the use of grammar for journalists working on *Guardian* publications. Smaller versions of such guides are often produced for use with visual material, such as logos and images in company or institution publications.

Conventions are often established in editorial design to give a publication a consistent identity. This relates to the house styles discussed earlier, and incorporates elements such as the positioning of captions relative to images, and style of page numbering.

Other considerations include where standard page information, such as page numbers or headers and footers, is positioned. In magazines and newspapers, page numbers are usually in the same place so that readers don't have problems finding them, and headers or footers may be used for specific parts of the publication. For example, the header for a lifestyle section would be different from the one used for a feature section.

All these conventions support the basic structure of a design and allow the designer to incorporate the various elements into a composition appropriate to the message that is being communicated.

Case Study
Reactype,
Parc&Maul

1.

At the initial ideas stage, the designers looked at letterforms in terms of producing abstract imagery, relating the imagery to background scenes in a particular setting. The installation was developed from earlier experiments with camera motion detection. The designers chose to use type as images because Reactype was to be shown at a typography exhibition. The example, right, from their workbook, shows an experiment with shapes formed by overlapping, outlined letterforms.

The hybrid theme was explored by creating hybrids between strikingly different elements. Parc&Maul looked at hybridization of contrasting typefaces: Baskerville (eighteenth-century English serif) and Franklin Gothic (twentieth-century American sans serif). They also looked at stationary and moving images by combining the static type grid with the moving images formed by the motion detector. This uses technology similar to that used to cause a light to turn on when something moves in its vicinity.

2.

In this further development the designers used the same letterform but in a far more structured way: the centre line was identified as a means of dividing the form and the areas within the letterform's outline – negative space – are looked at as shapes.

3.

The designers isolated parts of groups of letterforms, and looked at the shapes formed within the rectangles and the relationship between the various abstracted forms. The isolated areas are where they began to work out structure, based on computer-screen proportions (approximately 6:4).

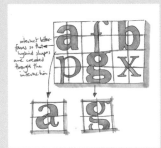

4.

This series shows the process of applying a simple grid to the letterforms, then drawing the reassembled shapes; the forms are still recognizable as letterforms. Again, the designers worked with standard ratios for screen design and experimented with how the forms fitted such proportions.

5.

The designers used rectangles to isolate areas and then looked at the intersection and combination of letterform shapes. The letterforms are becoming more abstracted as parts are removed. The rectangles are beginning to form a structure through the combination of shapes.

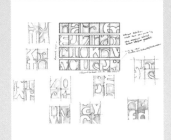

6.

Parc&Maul established a formal grid into which the abstracted letterforms would be fitted. Although the grid is quite rigid horizontally and vertically, the designers wanted to have a very fluid feel to the installation. The grid will provide an underpinning structure for the finished design.

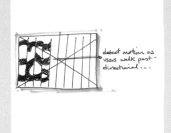

7.

The purpose of this sketch was to determine how the grid could be used to show the changes in a letterform when a viewer walks past the installation. This was worked out concurrently with the design of the structure as Parc&Maul were trying to identify how the images would react to user input.

Parc&Maul's brief was to produce a digital reactive media installation, Reactype, for the TypePlus exhibition that explored the theme of hybrid and the relationship between digital typography and image, motion detection and interactivity. The project was an experiment in alternative ways of interacting with a computer-based system that responds to movement. People interacting with the interface, in an exhibition space, may not be aware of their participation as the motion detector responds to the movements of anyone who passes it.

This project demonstrates the use of a formal structure to make a multimedia installation accessible. The underlying structure gives form to what would otherwise be a series of random images with no way of guiding the viewer.

8.

The letterforms were produced digitally and the grid is slightly less obvious with the structural lines taken out. This section is based on the Franklin Gothic typeface, and the letterforms have been treated as images although they are in alphabetical order.

9.

This is a screenshot of the work in the production stage, using the images formed from Baskerville letterforms. The horizontal rows of letters were moved to indicate how the design will work as an animation.

10.

This series of screenshots shows the finished installation with the fairly rigid structure of the cropped letterform images overlaid with the moving images captured by the camera and the software that interprets these images. Counterforms (the spaces left by the letterform shapes) in the images allow the colours captured by the camera (such as in people's clothes) to show through.

11.

This description of the work was produced for both print and screen. The designers used a multigrid in order to separate the two different pieces of text visually by putting them in columns of different widths, but at the same time linked the line of text that appears on the image to the body text.

In Reactype there is a strong link between print and screen with images designed for the screen used for the printed poster image, and the typefaces, Baskerville and Franklin Gothic, used in the body text of the poster.

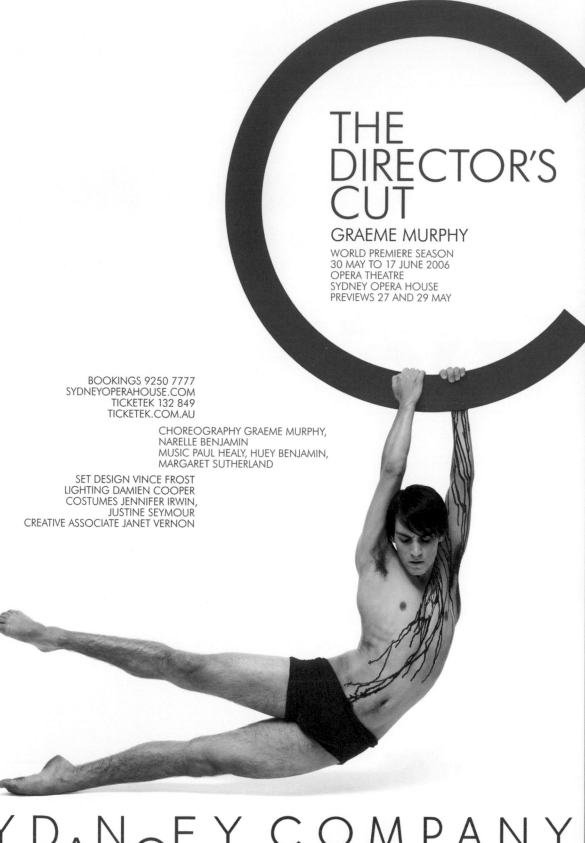

THE DIRECTOR'S CUT

GRAEME MURPHY

WORLD PREMIERE SEASON
30 MAY TO 17 JUNE 2006
OPERA THEATRE
SYDNEY OPERA HOUSE
PREVIEWS 27 AND 29 MAY

BOOKINGS 9250 7777
SYDNEYOPERAHOUSE.COM
TICKETEK 132 849
TICKETEK.COM.AU

CHOREOGRAPHY GRAEME MURPHY,
NARELLE BENJAMIN
MUSIC PAUL HEALY, HUEY BENJAMIN,
MARGARET SUTHERLAND

SET DESIGN VINCE FROST
LIGHTING DAMIEN COOPER
COSTUMES JENNIFER IRWIN,
JUSTINE SEYMOUR
CREATIVE ASSOCIATE JANET VERNON

SYDANCEY COMPANY

Composition

3

A layout is constructed to convey a message, and this chapter describes how, within this context, devices such as balance and imbalance, harmony and discord, symmetry and asymmetry can be used to communicate this message. It also discusses issues related to how the audience/reader find their way around a design.

Opposite: Frost Design have developed an unbalanced, somewhat unnerving composition in their design for the Sydney Dance Company.

What is Composition?

Composition is the arrangement and organization of the various elements of a design, such as text and images.

Composition can be a difficult concept for students to understand because it can come across as a complex web of rules and regulations; dos and don'ts. So, before launching into guidelines and suggestions, we would like to get something clear: the intention of composition is to make a design more effective.

You may find that you can work instinctively straight away or you may feel you need to look first at examples of other people's work. Through practice, you will develop the confidence to create powerful visual images and designs. As the creator of a design, you make the decisions as to what works best. Keep in mind that your ultimate goal is to communicate a message to your audience.

Jean-Benoît Lévy has used asymmetry to give this design an edgy feel which corresponds with the subject matter, the words and imagery used and the strange combination of the cloaked figure above an aerial view of what looks like suburban housing.

These posters for missing children are carefully balanced to reflect the serious nature of the message. At the same time, the images are chosen to attract attention.

Identifying the Audience

Organizing the various elements in a design is vital in communicating a message. Before this can be done, however, it is important to have a clear idea of the audience and the purpose of the communication. The location of the viewer or reader, or the way in which they will engage with an image may also affect their interpretation of the composition.

An example of the latter would be the use of an image in an advertising context, where two advertisements might be made for the same product: one as a poster for the side of a bus and the other for the inside of the same vehicle. The image in the poster is very large; because the audience is given very little time to read it as the bus passes, so the advertisement must be easily and quickly digested visually. In the second example, the viewer is a captive audience and has time to take in a more complex form of communication.

Identifying an audience is not always simple or straightforward. Often a message will be intended for a broad range of visual consumption, possibly by people of different nationalities or cultures. For instance, the poster shown to the right is designed by Nicola Chang for use in Hong Kong. Here, the cultural mix of East and West creates a complex problem where traditional assumptions about the way images are read cannot be counted on: the red and gold used in the poster are culturally significant in China (see Chapter 5) whereas the layout is in the Western format of left to right, top to bottom.

There is also the question of whether a message is serious or light-hearted. For example, if you were designing an advertisement for painkillers, you would want it to convey the message that they have a calming/soothing effect, not that they would make anyone who used them aggravated or anxious. Here the feel of the composition comes into play; a design that looks off-balance may be interpreted as upbeat whereas one that is symmetrical may give the impression of being solemn.

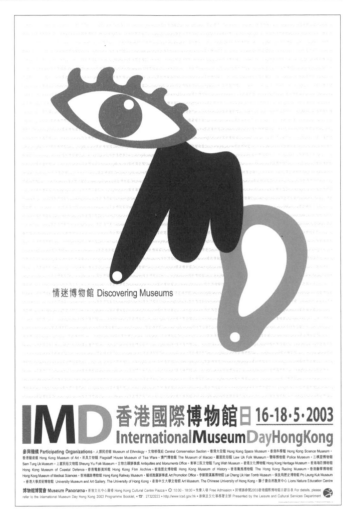

Banner designed by Nicola Chang for the Hong Kong Science Museum.

The Rules
of Composition

Whatever rules you are given, they may have to be broken at
some time or other. The rules used in composition work in
the same way that a grid provides structure for a page layout:
as guides.

One of the first considerations when deciding on the
composition of a layout is the effect you are trying to create. For
example, is it intended to give a calm impression or a disturbing
one? The way its elements are arranged – symmetrically or
asymmetrically, for instance – can affect the way it is seen.

Symmetry and asymmetry

A symmetrical layout is generally considered to be more
traditional, stable and calming than an asymmetrical one, which
may appear more edgy and disturbing, particularly if it is
unbalanced. A symmetrical layout is one where, if you draw
a line down the centre of a page, the right side of the line
mirrors the left side. ❶

An asymmetrical design helps to create tension and contrast;
it upsets people's sense of order and equilibrium by causing
an imbalance. However, it is useful to remember that it can still
have equal weighting – the balance of content on each side of
the design. ❷

❶ This web design by Bunch Design is symmetrical. Even though both sides are not exact
mirrors of each other, the balance of each side is equal.

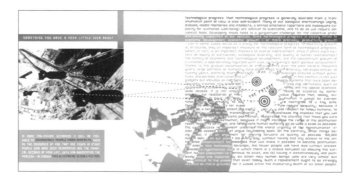

❷ This design by Kate Tutunik uses asymmetry to convey an edgy, unbalanced feel.

Design two posters or web promotions for a play or concert. The component parts include an image, a title, the dates, location and cost. One design must be symmetrical, the other asymmetrical. The scale of the individual components may differ between the designs.

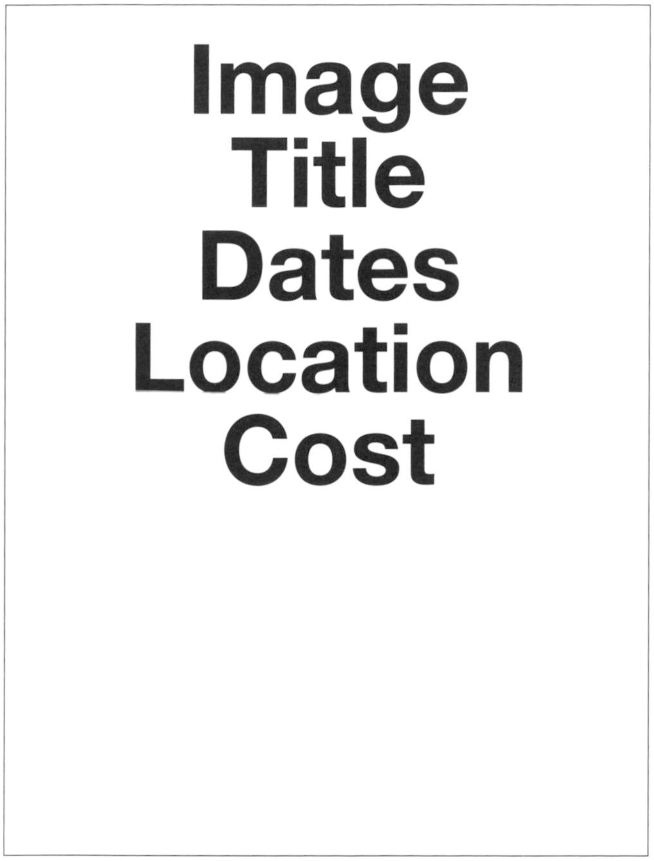

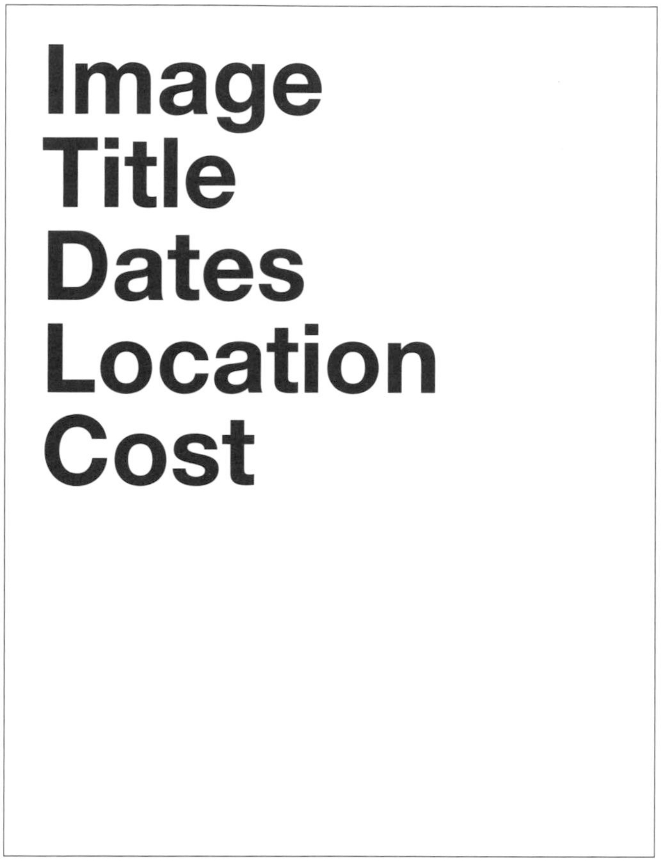

Image
Title
Dates
Location
Cost

Image
Title
Dates
Location
Cost

Image
Title
Dates
Location
Cost

Image
Title
Dates
Location
Cost

Fresh

(Mint)

Unpretentious

(Vanilla)

Team player

(Neopolitian)

Crowd pleaser

(Chocolate)

Lateral thinking

(White Chocolate)

Commitment

(After Eight)

Open-minded

(Curry)

Sharp wit

(Lemon Sorbet)

Reliable

(Strawberry)

Full of surprises

(Tutti Frutti)

The odd slip-up

(Banana)

Well rounded

(Melon)

Software skills

(Apple Sorbet)

Show-off

*(Belgian double chocolate,
marshmallow, fudge delight)*

Ambitious

(Passionfruit)

Work hard, play hard

(Rum & Raisin)

Pithy

(Orange)

From Cornwall

(Clotted Cream)

Tireless

(Coffee)

The finishing touch

(Cherry)

Portfolio Tasting

BA(Hons) Graphic Design Reception

6:30–10:30pm Wednesday 7th May 2008

The Vaults, Royal Society of Arts, 8 John Adam Street
(Durham House St. entrance), London, WC2N 6EZ

RSVP: Jon Unwin, Course Leader. jonu@falmouth.ac.uk

University College
FALMOUTH
Incorporating Dartington College of Arts

❶ The design shown opposite has a
balanced and harmonious feel because the
shapes are all similar and of a similar size.
There is nothing jarring or off-balance, and
the unusual use of ice-cream in relation to
the text prevents the design being boring.

Harmony and discord

Order and equilibrium or tension and contrast can be created
using harmony and discord. Harmony can give a calm, passive,
still impression whereas the use of discord can result in feelings
of disturbance and uneasiness. (Harmony and discord in colour
are discussed in Chapter 5.)

A harmonious composition may be one where all the images
are a similar type or size, whereas a discordant one may contain
images that contradict each other and are therefore not balanced.
❶

Balance

Balance relates to symmetry and asymmetry, and harmony
and discord, but may also refer to the relationship between
text and images or the various graphic elements on a page.
For example, if a page has even amounts of text and images
it may appear more balanced than one with far more text than
images. How balance is used in a design is dependent on
readership or audience: in a serious publication an equal balance
of text and image may appear too light and, vice versa, in a
light-hearted article an equal balance of text and image may
appear too serious. Balance may be applied across a double-
page spread or, indeed, across a publication where the style
of the publication requires a constant, balanced overall feel.

 Take care as the use of balanced composition across a publication
could end up looking boring.

Even though all the action is centred on the right-hand side of this poster by Amirali
Ghasemi, the design achieves balance through the use of a darker colour on the left half
of the poster and because the heads of both people point to the left-hand side. Also, the
white wavy lines are more visible against the darker background on the left and this pulls
your eye towards that side.

Opposite: in this manuscript the balance between type and image has been carefully considered with the main image leading into the text, balanced by flamboyant flourishes and decoration.

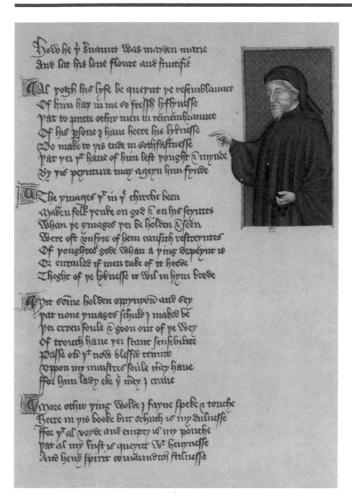

This manuscript page design is very simple, using white space around the text and image which helps to draw the reader to the information. This is helped by the illustration, which directs the reader into the text using the body language of the figure.

In early manuscripts, both Eastern and Western, there is a careful balance between type and image. This may be the result of tried and tested solutions or conventions, but it could also be down to individual monks and scribes, and their particular quirks. It is useful to remember this and avoid following any current trend in layout and composition styles. Experiment and develop your own solutions. Look at the work of well-known designers such as Fletcher or The Designers Republic: none of them were followers of prevailing fashions. However, great designers often used tried and tested methods (even if they didn't use them in the style of their contemporaries) and these can always, or nearly always, be relied upon. Examples of these include the Fibonacci series or golden section.

If you only mimic the current style, your work will only ever be restyling or imitation. If you take risks or think otherwise, the results may not always work but you will have expressed individuality and your own quirks, and therefore bucked the trend – you will stand out. Do not fall into the trap of overusing the latest gimmick or trick that the developers of the latest software provide, just because you can.

Fibonacci series/golden section

The Fibonacci series is named after the nineteenth-century
Italian mathematician, Leonardo Fibonacci, who discovered
it, and is simply a series of numbers produced when each
number is the sum of the preceding two.

The series – for example, 2, 3, 5, 8, 13, 21, 34, 55, 89,
144, 233 – is important because each pair of numbers in the
series has a proportional relationship of roughly 8:13, which
is known as the golden section. The ancient Greeks knew this,
and used the golden section to achieve harmonious and
beautiful proportions.

Although there is a mathematical logic to the Fibonacci
numbers, their importance to artists and designers is in the
aesthetic relationships they create within a composition. Using
these relationships may be considered a quick and almost
infallible route to a balanced design.

Activity

To create a series of Fibonacci rectangles and a Fibonacci spiral, draw two small squares together, then draw another square using the combined lengths of the two squares as one side. Keep repeating this, as in the diagram. You can see from the proportion of these rectangles that they relate to the standardized United Kingdom paper sizes A4, A3, A2, A1 and A0.

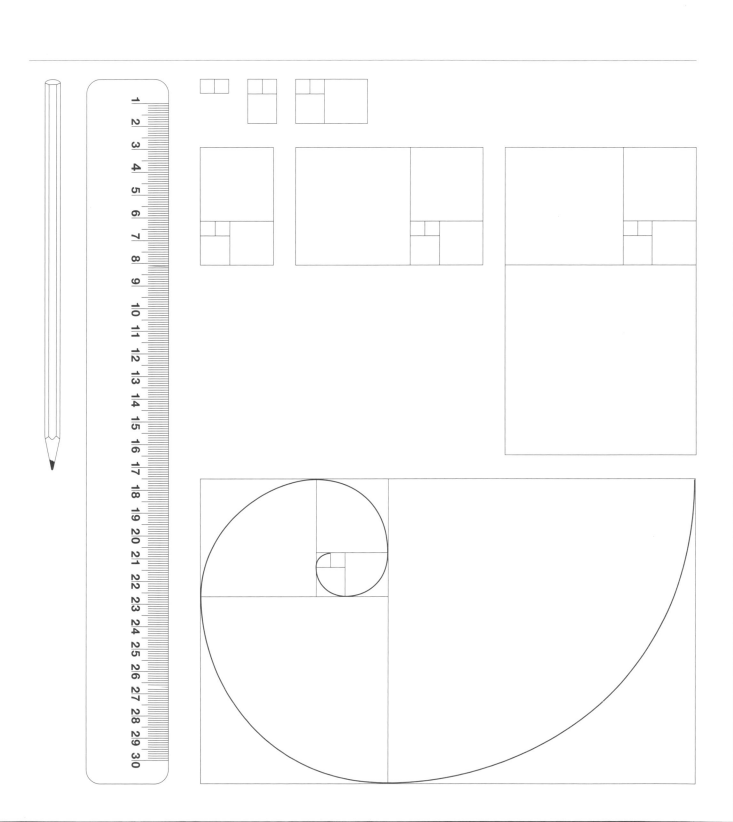

Activity

To form a golden section, draw a square then divide it into two equal sections vertically. Now draw a diagonal line from the bottom of the middle line to the top right-hand corner of the right-hand section to form a triangle. Using a compass, draw a circle, the centre of which is the bottom of the middle line. The radius of the circle should be aligned to the top of the triangle you created and should, if drawn correctly, also touch the top left-hand corner of your square. Extend the baseline of your square to intersect the circle on the right. If you draw a vertical line from this intersection, you should be able to complete the rectangle by extending the top line to meet it. You should now have a diagram of a golden section as shown in the example.

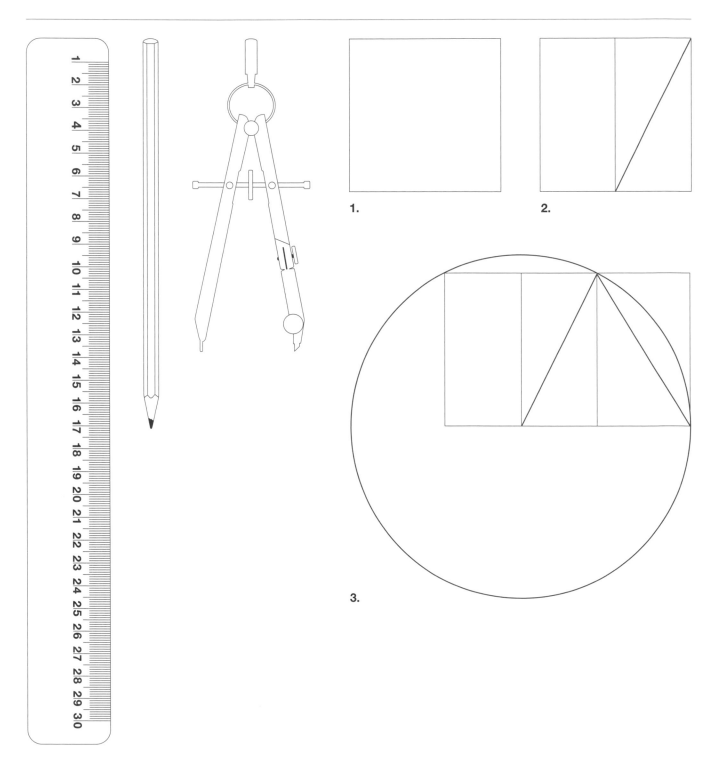

1.

2.

3.

The rule of thirds

Another way of dividing up a design is through the rule of thirds. This is simpler to apply than the golden section and is often used by photographers. The image area is divided into thirds and the grid lines cross each other creating active areas that stand out. Key information is placed in and around the hotspots, where the lines intersect, to draw the audience in.

Related to the rule of thirds is the way interior stylists recommend that artefacts should be arranged in groups of three. A group of three objects generally appears more pleasing than an arrangement of two or four. It is commonplace in interior design magazines to see a row of three pictures hanging on a wall or a row of three identical vases; it is an easy solution that most people respond to. The grouping of objects in odd numbers rather than even is also an effective way of implying randomness or chance in compositions such as still lifes, so that they appear natural rather than staged.

A grid that divides the image into thirds has been laid over this photograph in order to demonstrate the area of activity at the intersection of the lines in the top right of the image.

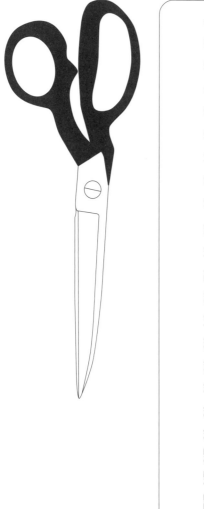

In the following examples, several sections of text have been printed out and cut into a variety of sizes, then used together with slabs of colour, images cut from magazines and scrap photographs. The object of the exercise is to experiment quickly and easily with a range of possibilities relating to the sort of layout you hope to achieve.

You can use anything that comes to hand, such as sections from leaflets or brochures, or even objects such as buttons, paperclips or fabric flowers. Bear in mind that it is useful to use things that are appropriate to the message. So, for example, if gardening is the subject of a design, images of plants, flowers and gardening tools would be appropriate. It is also useful to cut the images to a size appropriate to your grid. ❶

As an alternative method, you could scan or download images and text, and work with them on screen, using an appropriate design software package.

Cutting up different shapes such as circles and triangles can help you to think differently, or from a different viewpoint, and provide exciting opportunities. ❷

To experiment further or in a less controlled way, try dropping assorted cut-outs on to a sheet of paper, then experiment with the resulting shapes and patterns. This can provide an extra dimension and more interest as some pieces will fall across the edges of the paper or overlap each other. ❸

❶

In this picture, the images and text being moved around relate to different types of flower and therefore a fairly simple structure is used to convey a passive layout.

In this second picture, the content is downhill biking and therefore about action and movement so the designer is experimenting with a more active combination of text and images.

❷

This image shows an experiment with a variety of shapes, taken from pictures and pieces of coloured paper.

❸

The designer is dropping cut-out shapes on to an empty layout.

Once the pieces have fallen, the designer can start arranging them to see what ideas come from the resulting shapes and patterns.

❶ Martin Woodtli's design shown
opposite is striking and contradictory
as the arm is much larger than both
the object supporting it and the people.

Scale

Changes in scale may have the opposite effect to odd-number
groupings in that they can make people look twice at a design.
Scale and variation in scale are useful in reinforcing a message
or information. For example, a mixture of large and small
images creates a sense of activity or liveliness. Several images
that are all the same size may have less impact than one large
image and several small ones.

Scale also provides hierarchy and guides the audience.
In much the same way that the type in the title of an article is
usually larger than that used for the body text, so a larger
image can help direct the reader or viewer to the most important
part of a message. A large image (or a small one) used effectively
can change the whole emphasis of a design. Using scale
in this way is useful if the design contains both a main and a
subsidiary message. ❶

Using items of different sizes may also provide reference
points. If a cut-out picture of a plant has no context, it is difficult
for the audience to see its size or be impressed because it
could be either small or large. If the plant is placed next to
something that is identifiable as being a certain size, such as
a sparrow, this provides the scale and the drama of the plant's
size is conveyed to the reader or viewer.

Not all differences in scale need to be dramatic, but very
subtle differences may not be noticeable and result in a design
having a still, inactive feel. Sometimes a subdued, static feeling
may be intentional (you wouldn't want a poster for a remembrance
event to look particularly active) and sometimes extreme stillness
provides a contrast to an area of activity – this is another
useful device for gaining attention.

Poster design often uses scale, usually featuring a large
image or word-as-image that dominates the design and
draws the audience into the actual message. This image may
supplement the main message, support it or sometimes
replace it altogether. It can fight with the message (a discordant
composition) or work with it (a harmonious one).

A very large image of a small object, such as a fly, could
attract attention as the fly would look quite different dominating
a large poster than it would at normal size. But a small fly in
a large empty space (white space) could also be very effective.

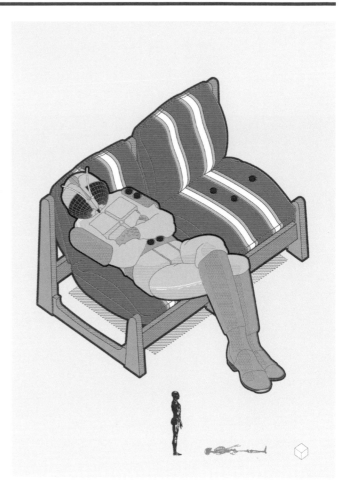

Martin Woodtli has used discord between message and image by seating a strange figure
on the sofa in order to draw attention to the design.

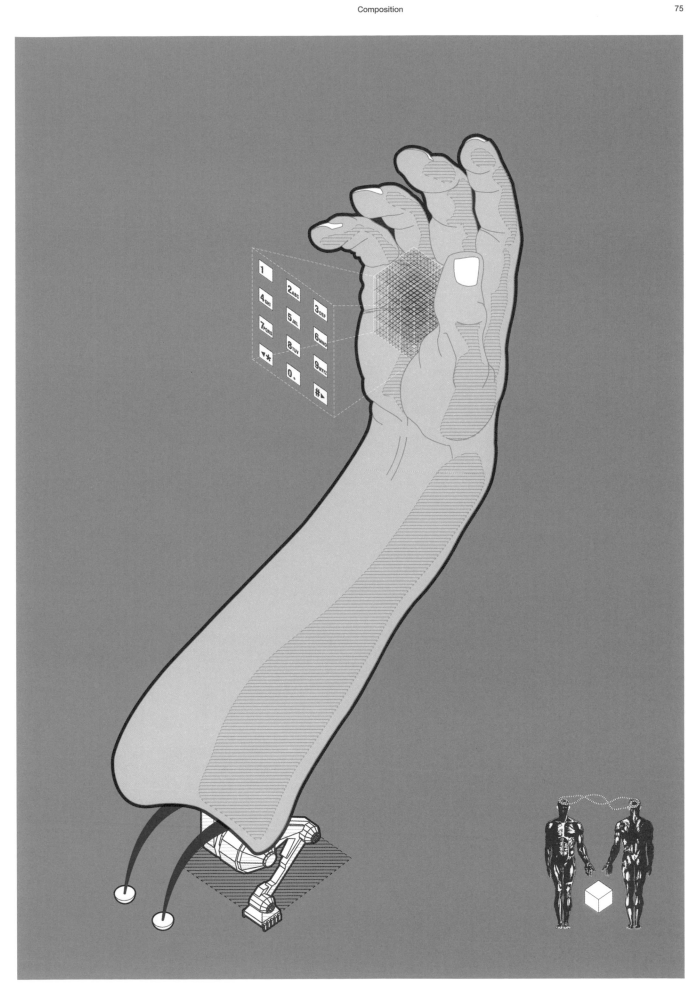

In Ludovic Balland's poster, the image of
Warsaw works in harmony with the text
which is about a person's memories of
this city.

MUZEUM
sztuki
nowoczesnej
w warszawie

wydarzenie

: 5 grudnia od 18.00 do 24.00
na północnym dziedzińcu Pałacu Kultury i Nauki,
obok przyszłego placu budowy gmachu Muzeum.

POMARAŃCZOWY   CZERWONY   JASNONIEBIESKI   CZERWONY   FIOLETOWY   NIEBIESKI   NIEBIESKI   ŻÓŁTY   ZIELONY

PHOTOGRAPHY AND DESIGN, LUDOVIC BALLAND

Pokazem „9 promieni światła na niebie"
chcemy przypomnieć mieszkańcom
Warszawy wyjątkowego artystę i wyjątkowego warszawiaka. Henryk Stażewski
urodził się tu w 1894 roku i to tu przeżył
94 fascynujące lata. Był rówieśnikiem
nowoczesnego świata i nowoczesnej
sztuki. Za jego sprawą u progu lat 20.,
wraz z niepodległością zawitał do Polski
ruch awangardowy. Tworzył obrazy,
plakaty, projekty wnętrz i scenografie
teatralne, zawsze podporządkowane
geometrii. Wystawiał swe projekty w
salonach automobilowych, bo to one
były wówczas świątyniami nowoczesno-
ści. Współpracował z Pietem Mondria-
nem, a Kazimierzowi Malewiczowi
urządził pierwszą poza Rosją wystawę –
w 1927 roku w warszawskim Hotelu
Polonia. W latach 60. zamieszkał w
pracowni na dachu bloku przy Al. Świer-
czewskiego, dzisiejszej Al. Solidarności.
Codziennie od godziny 6 rano do 11
malował, następnie wyruszał autobusem
do kawiarni Stowarzyszenia Architektów
Polskich przy ulicy Foksal, gdzie czekali
na niego wielbiciele, zaś przed godziną
17 wracał do swej pracowni i otwierał
salon - prawdziwe centrum warszawskie-
go życia artystycznego.
Wymyślone przez Henryka Stażewskiego
malarstwo na niebie, które 5 grudnia
obejrzą warszawiacy, po raz pierwszy
zostało pokazane 9 maja 1970 roku we
Wrocławiu. Do potrzeb obecnego
pokazu w Warszawie projekt dostosował
współpracownik Stażewskiego,
artysta Jan Chwałczyk

Henryk Stażewski

9promieni
światła
na niebie

Activity

Transpose an image from one design to another, setting it in a different context. For example, take an image used in a wedding magazine spread, such as a bouquet or bridesmaid, and transpose it to an advertisement for a combine harvester. Or take an image from a science fiction comic and transpose it to a classical music CD cover.

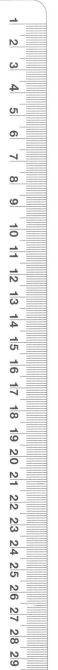

The image of the market stallholder scratching his head has been transposed to another context and now looks as if he is lost or is wondering what the building in the woods is.

❶ This double-page spread from a
Norwegian planning document by
Grandpeople demonstrates how effective
white space can be in signalling the
importance of the image and text and,
in this case, making the design look
clean and sparse.

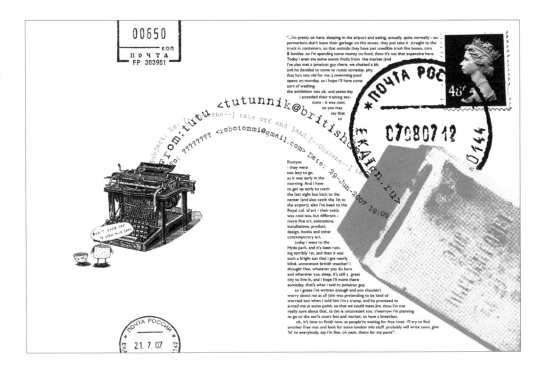

❷ This design by Kate Tutunik, for a
double-page spread in a magazine, uses
an image that bleeds off to the right to
suggest that the object extends beyond
the boundaries of the page and is forcing
itself into the design, therefore leading
the reader into the text.

This design by Madelyn Postman makes use of white space to outline the shapes of the objects and text, and to relate the negative space on the outside to the space on the inside of the group, resulting in a powerful, lively composition.

White space

White space, or space with nothing in it, is seen as wasted space in newspaper design (not the advertisements that appear in them), where it is usually considered a luxury. This perception is useful as white space, used carefully, can certainly convey a feeling of luxury or spaciousness.

White space may also be useful in a design that requires a feeling of calm or emptiness, or as a distraction from large sections of text.

This empty, unused, negative space can help to establish hierarchy as it signals the importance of the elements it surrounds: an item with lots of white space around it seems more important than one surrounded by no white space. ❶

White space provides breathing room for the elements of a design. It is not common in early designs, for example that of the sixteenth century up to the Victorian period, whereas it is used more often in modern ones, where it may simply be large margins in a magazine or borders around images, which help to frame them. White, or negative, space is as important as the elements (positive space) that it surrounds. It provides a pause or even creates a pattern or device to engage the reader.

Bleed

In the same way that white space can create a feeling of spaciousness, so can the use of bleed. This is where the information (image or text) extends further than the edge of the design space (physical or virtual). In print, the design space is the area within the trim marks that indicate where a page is to be cut. In web design, it is usually defined by the screen edges. ❷

 When using bleed in a printed document, you need to be careful to allow some extra image (around 3 mm / ⅛ in) to extend beyond the edge of the printed page, so that when it is trimmed you do not end up with an edge that shows the page colour if the page is cut incorrectly.

Bleed can be very useful for suggesting that there is more of an image than is visible or to lead a reader on to the next page. Certain images are appropriate for bleed and others are not. For example, it would look odd if a picture of a house was bled off the page, chopping off part of it and making it unrecognizable. Likewise, it is important to keep contextual information where this is relevant – if the outer support in a picture of a bridge went missing it could look as if the bridge were floating in space. However, if a picture of a galaxy is bled off the printed area it could suggest infinite space by implying that there is more there than the reader can see.

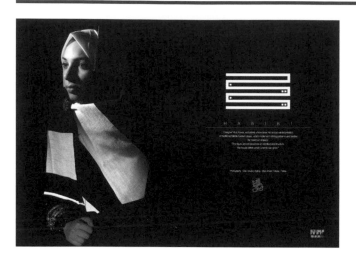

❶ In this design by Muiz Anwar the person is looking out of the page to the left, but the strong typographic element in white pulls the viewer back to the right-hand page.

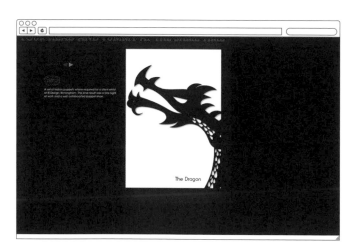

❷ In this screenshot from Sean Bird's web site, the dragon is facing towards the information, drawing the viewer into the page.

Tension

Using bleed can create tension as it can help to direct the eye to other elements in a design. Tension is concerned with the relationship between elements and the way they relate to the virtual or physical limits of the design. For example, if an image of a person is facing off the page and bled off, this creates tension as it directs the viewer out of the design space. In order to pull the viewer back in, you would need an element that directs them back to the main part of the design. (The way the viewer is directed around a design is discussed below.) This use of an image to create tension can help create a very dynamic design. ❶ ❷

Closure

Similar to the way in which bleed suggests more, closure leads the viewer to assume there is a missing part of something, such as an image or title, or assume a part is missing. It may also be used as a device to create a more interesting layout. The easiest way of demonstrating how closure works is to look at the letter C which, on its own, may be perceived as an O or a round shape as we naturally complete the circle. One of the most frequent uses of closure is on magazine covers where the head, or a part, of the person or people in the image used obliterates a letter or letters of the magazine's title (masthead).

People usually complete a missing part in the same way as they navigate a page: without knowing they are doing it. ❸

❸ Jason Munn makes effective use of closure in this design where we read the images as discs as well as reading the word 'why'.

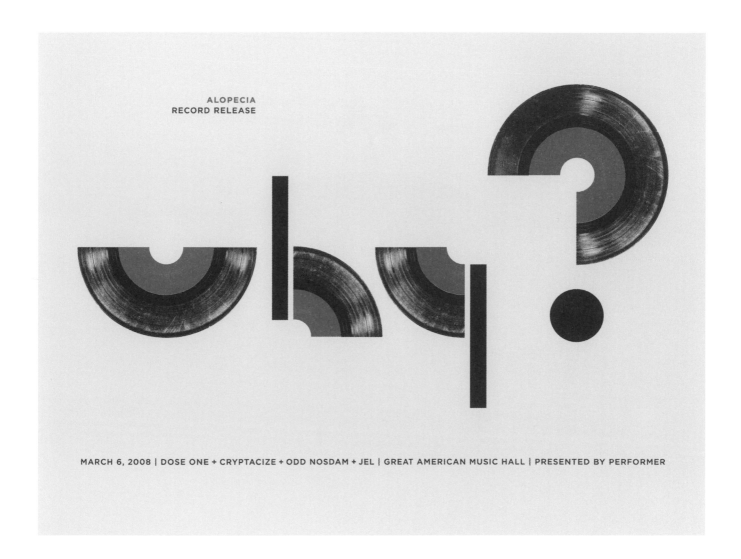

❶ In this design Jason Munn has used
the top third (well, slightly more) of the
image to draw the audience in. The island
is also pointing to this top third, reinforcing
its importance.

Directing the Audience

Elements of a design are used to help viewers to navigate through the information so that the message is clearly communicated. Although there is seldom anything as obvious as a signpost directing them to the left or right, this is what the designer is trying to do – direct viewers around the design.

When designing a composition, it is useful to know how to help people navigate through the information. How does the eye travel around the page and how is it led to important things?

People in most Western countries read from left to right and top to bottom, and for this reason, when you are designing for an audience in the West the best position for important elements is the top third of the page, and specifically the left-hand corner. Anecdotally, a friend who worked in catalogue design was always told to put hard-to-sell items top left, which is similar to supermarkets putting items they want to shift on the ends of aisles. Remember, though, that the Western way of reading is not the case in other parts of the world. ❶

  Don't lead the eye off the page unless you do it deliberately to lead the reader on to the next page/part of a book or article.

You can direct a viewer around a composition by use of various devices such as balance, graphic symbols and hierarchy as in the example shown above right, where Sahra Mesgna has composed the various elements in an imbalanced way to help direct the viewer to the information. So, for example, something in the foreground may lead or point you to the main content. The most obvious trick is the shocking/stunning image that stops you in your tracks and encourages you to read the article or find out what it is advertising.

Sahra Mesgna directs the viewer to the main message by use of a strong image and items that direct the eye through the information.

It is noticeable that in television interviews, if someone is talking but not looking directly at the camera there is always a space, either to the left or the right, for them to look into as if someone is there. In print, a picture that shows a person looking out of a page directs the reader away from the content or message – but if the picture shows the person looking into a page, it directs the reader in. Someone looking out of a right-hand page, to the right, can direct the reader to the next (left-hand) page. However, if they are looking out of a left-hand page, to the left, the reader is led off the page – and backwards through the book or magazine. A picture of a person looking down from top left and/or a person looking up from bottom right of a page directs the reader into the information contained in the page.

  Avoid leading the reader's eye off the page before you've got your message across.

A good example of how to direct readers is commonly found in double-page spreads in magazines, where an image often dominates the right-hand page. This suggests to readers that there is something of interest there as they flick through and draws them in. The image will have been carefully selected so that it directs them to the left-hand page where the title and text sit. It is important that something within the image leads readers to the left-hand page, and that an element on this page, usually the title, ties them into the information. ❶

The use of a strong image in the centre of a page, surrounded by blocks of text and subsidiary images, can also be effective: the central image acts as the visual draw as well as unifying the composition.

Images speak louder than words

When designing a composition it is important to remember that the first thing the reader understands is the image; text always comes second. So it is sensible to make the image do the work. For example, if the title is the most important information to be communicated, the reader could be navigated/directed to look at it first by the use of an image that directs the eye towards it.

Often the image and title, or main text, are the most obvious parts of a design and the key to drawing readers in. Examples are newspapers where the front page is dominated by a key image and headline and web pages where splash, introductory or opening pages often have minimal information but use images or images-and-title to draw people in and get them to click to enter the site.

In web design, as in magazine and book design, navigation is essential and images can play an important part in this. Visual metaphor is often used, probably the most obvious being a picture of a house representing the home page. A parallel in print is the use of printers' graphic devices such as scissors and a dotted line (broken rule) for cut, or printer's fingers used as pointers. These obvious pointers are used to connect different elements but there are more subtle ways of achieving this. ❷

Joel Stone's poster uses a tightly cropped portrait, with the man looking at the information at the base of the poster, directing the viewer towards the main information.

Continuity

Connections may be suggested by various means, such as grouping images or presenting them together in a way that implies they are interrelated or connected. For example, a group of images that are all the same size indicates that they are related to each other.

Grouping elements to form repetition or rhythm is pleasing but can become boring – the technique is effective but needs to be used carefully. For example, a certain amount of repetition is used in magazines. Margins are often consistent, page numbers are in the same place or there is consistent use of headers and/or footers. However, if all the pages were constructed in the same way the publication could look boring, so magazines usually use a variety of layouts and compositions but with common basic themes such as width of margins and the positioning of page numbers.

❶ Daniel Morgenstern's large image on the right-hand page faces the title, directing the reader inward towards the content.

כשהיה מישאל חשין בן שלוש הוא נהג להסתובב בבית ולהוציא את מלאי האנרגיות והכעסים שלו על צעצועים ורהיטים, עד שאמו נאלצה לקשור אותו במושכות. עשרות שנים לאחר מכן, כשהתמנה אחרי מאבק ממושך לעליון, היו אלה המערערים, הסנגורים ואפילו חבריו לכס המשפט שנכוו ממזגו הסוער ומלשונו החריפה. הפעם לא היה מי שירתום לו מושכות, אפילו לא יריבו משכבר הימים הנשיא ברק. משה גורלי מסכם את כהונתו של השופט הכי צבעוני בבית המשפט העליון, שלא חס על דתיים ועל אישי ציבור, אך נמס מול קורבנות ובעלי חיים

משה גורלי

איור: דניאל מורגנשטרן

❷ Phillip Skinner uses a broken rule to indicate where a ticket should be torn.

Relating Images
to Text

This sign uses a strong image to alert people and uses text to explain the nature
of the danger and support the warning symbol.

As mentioned earlier, people usually observe visual information
before text, so using images with text can engage the viewer
more effectively as they are drawn towards the visual. For
example, warning signs usually use an image to alert people
and there may be further information in the form of text.

Using images with text may allow the designer to be more
adventurous as there are diverse elements to play with; on a
magazine double-page spread there could be images, title, body
text, pull quotes and information bars. All of these are separate
elements to be organized into a piece of visual communication.

There are different ways of looking at the text and image
combination. Text can be supplemented with images, or it can
be replaced with image(s). Both can be very effective. In terms
of communication, it is not usually effective to use images and
text that both say the same thing as this not only provides
superfluous information but is also confusing, and may be seen
as being patronizing.

Combining images with text is not to be confused with their
use in the interpretation of text, as in an illustrated book where
images are used to aid the understanding of the narrative.

We read images rather than text, and we read text as shapes
that the words form rather than as individual letters, which is
why text in capital letters is more difficult to read. This was
brought home to us when a friend described her experience
when travelling on the Moscow underground. She doesn't
understand Russian and all the station names are in capital
letters, which looked the same so there was no visual trigger
to help her differentiate between one station and another.
Similarly, sections of text can be seen as blocks or shapes that
the designer uses as another visual element in a design.

Shades of grey

As well as shape, text has what designers call 'colour'. This is
down to the density of the body text, which may be affected
by typeface, typestyle, weight, width, size, line spacing and
letter spacing, and is referred to as shades of grey as well as
the colour of type. If you squint at a page of text, you lose the
words and get an overall impression of a grey block; this is
a design element in just the same way that an image is. The
block of text needs to be considered in relation to all the other
elements in terms of its tone or greyness. ❶

When laying out text be aware of the negative space or shapes
that are created.

Don't make the mistake that one of us did early in her career: she set
up a double-page spread with black-and-white images of landscape;
the balance of text and images was almost equal and she selected the
typeface appropriate to the content (Gill Sans). But she then decided
that on screen this typeface looked a little dark with the pictures, so
she changed it to Gill Sans Light – and as a bonus had the opportunity
to increase the size of one of the images as Gill Sans Light takes up
less space. It looked good on screen, as did the inkjet proof, but not
so good when it came back from the printers: the type was far too pale
and was completely dominated by the images – no balance.

❶ This diagram shows the variations in colour of type, or shades of grey, caused by using different typefaces and variations in type style in the left-hand column and line spacing (leading) in the right-hand column.

This is an example of how you achieve different shades of grey in blocks of text by varying the typeface, type style, weight, width, size letter spacing and line spacing. For example, this section of text is in Gill Sans Light, size 9pt with 11pt line spacing.

This is an example of how you achieve different shades of grey in blocks of text by varying the typeface, type style, weight, width, size letter spacing and line spacing. For example, this section of text is in Gill Sans Light Italic, size 9pt with 11pt line spacing.

This is an example of how you achieve different shades of grey in blocks of text by varying the typeface, type style, weight, width, size letter spacing and line spacing. For example, this section of text is in Gill Sans Regular, size 9pt with 11pt line spacing.

This is an example of how you achieve different shades of grey in blocks of text by varying the typeface, type style, weight, width, size letter spacing and line spacing. For example, this section of text is in Gill Sans Italic, size 9pt with 11pt line spacing.

This is an example of how you achieve different shades of grey in blocks of text by varying the typeface, type style, weight, width, size letter spacing and line spacing. For example, this section of text is in Gill Sans Bold, size 9pt with 11pt line spacing.

This is an example of how you achieve different shades of grey in blocks of text by varying the typeface, type style, weight, width, size letter spacing and line spacing. For example, this section of text is in Gill Sans Bold Italic, size 9pt with 11pt line spacing.

This is an example of how you achieve different shades of grey in blocks of text by varying the typeface, type style, weight, width, size letter spacing and line spacing. For example, this section of text is in Gill Sans Ultra Bold, size 9pt with 11pt line spacing.

This is an example of how you achieve different shades of grey in blocks of text by varying the typeface, type style, weight, width, size letter spacing and line spacing. For example, this section of text is in Baskerville Regular, size 9pt with 24pt line spacing.

This is an example of how you achieve different shades of grey in blocks of text by varying the typeface, type style, weight, width, size letter spacing and line spacing. For example, this section of text is in Baskerville Regular, size 9pt with 20pt line spacing.

This is an example of how you achieve different shades of grey in blocks of text by varying the typeface, type style, weight, width, size letter spacing and line spacing. For example, this section of text is in Baskerville Regular, size 9pt with 16pt line spacing.

This is an example of how you achieve different shades of grey in blocks of text by varying the typeface, type style, weight, width, size letter spacing and line spacing. For example, this section of text is in Baskerville Regular, size 9pt with 13pt line spacing.

This is an example of how you achieve different shades of grey in blocks of text by varying the typeface, type style, weight, width, size letter spacing and line spacing. For example, this section of text is in Baskerville Regular, size 9pt with 11pt line spacing.

This is an example of how you achieve different shades of grey in blocks of text by varying the typeface, type style, weight, width, size letter spacing and line spacing. For example, this section of text is in Baskerville Regular, size 9pt with 9pt line spacing.

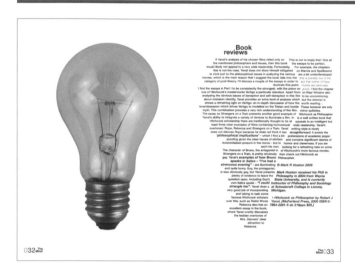

For this double-page spread Josh Gidman has cut out the lightbulb and then filled in its shape with text, which he has then run around with a section of text.

Runaround (or text wrap)

The colour of blocks of text is important when text follows the outline of an image to which it relates in order to maintain the intended relationship between the two: known as runaround. This device, also called text wrap, is used to create variety in text. However, text and image combinations like this should not be overused as they risk losing their impact or effectiveness. Runaround can make a clear link between the written components and images in a design.

Attak used cut-out techniques to provide impact in this poster design.

Cut-out or spot images

Cut-out images or spot illustrations have been used effectively since medieval scribes used them at the beginning of manuscripts to illustrate the content. Cut-outs from images, such as a flowerhead cropped from a bunch of flowers, can be an effective way of drawing attention to, or highlighting, an element in a design.

Colour linking

Another method of linking written elements to images is to select a colour from an image and use it for some or all of the text. Obviously, it's necessary to be very careful as some colours will not work well in body text: yellow text on a white page would be very difficult to read. However, yellow on a black background would be easier and this leads to the importance of the background and its colour in a composition. Although unused areas of a design are referred to as white space, they could be any colour. When you use a background colour, think of it as an element in the design and ensure that it works well with the other elements and contributes to the message. A pale pink background to an article about a war, for example, would not work.

The use of an unframed box that contains a light tint of colour is a subtle way of isolating an item in a design or giving it more importance. This device can also be used to link independent but related items.

Framing

When relating images and text, or any combination of elements in a design, there is sometimes a temptation to isolate items by framing them. In moderation, this can be a useful device for indicating the importance of an item or its independence from the main body of the design. However, the thicker or stronger the frame, the more it becomes an element in its own right, which may lead to it dominating the composition. This also applies to devices such as thick rules or other framing elements such as patterns. ❶

Framing, like all the methods of composition described in this chapter, can be used to communicate with the audience. We have outlined the considerations you will need to take into account when thinking about the composition of a design. Many of the issues discussed, such as navigation and the relationship between image and text, are influenced by the message a design is intended to convey.

It is worth remembering that although a composition in print often has to grab the reader's attention quickly, web or digital composition needs to work even more effectively as people click through. To a certain extent, magazines and books are still about relatively relaxed reading whereas the web seems to be synonymous with instant communication and finding things easily.

❶ Attak used white to frame sections of text, identifying them as being separate from the image but linking them together using colour.

Case Study
Juvelen 1,
Grandpeople

1.

These preliminary hand-drawn sketches show how ideas for layout, and the shapes and typefaces to be incorporated in the designs, were generated.

2.

Strong, uppercase type was required to work with the shapes that were generated. These are examples of the sort of typographic material Grandpeople used for reference.

3.

These images were developed using illustration software based on the original hand-drawn images. The software enabled the designer to achieve clean, controlled lines and finishes, and to experiment with the shapes reversed out of black as well as black on white. It also provided the opportunity to manipulate the shapes – for example, by rotating and resizing – quickly and easily. As the shapes were refined, it became clear that they draw on Surrealist images.

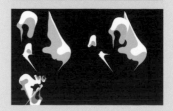

Grandpeople were commissioned to design a booklet and cover for an album, Juvelen 1, by Juvelen, a Swedish pop- and club-music artist. The brief was to produce something that was dark and alluring but avoided the obvious picture of the artist's face on the cover. Juvelen did not want the design to have a strong pop culture feel, but rather a 'special, strange and just a bit commercial' look.

The designers looked at a combination of text and images, seeking to create a fusion of magazine and scientific-publication design. They wanted Juvelen to appear to be 'the bold headliner of his own glossy magazine', but with very little extra information other than his name spread throughout the pages of the booklet. This case study has been chosen because it illustrates how the designers have considered the arrangement of images and text to communicate the feel associated with Juvelen. They have considered many aspects of composition including audience, symmetry and asymmetry, white space and cut-out images.

The designers sought to develop a logo that would act as a visual identity for Juvelen as well as working well with the images in the composition for the CD cover's layout.

4.

The designers experimented with drawing the letterforms, based on reference material, before using software to develop a finished typeface.

5.

A logo was part of the brief, and these four images show stages in the development of its design.

6.

This image shows one of the designers' experiments with combining the finished logo design with the finalized shapes for the cover design. Grandpeople wanted to achieve a visual balance between the two. The larger of the images is the Juvelen logo and, in order to maintain a balance, they have coloured it a subtle tone of grey that makes it sink slightly into the background and prevents it dominating the composition when juxtaposed with the smaller fluid shapes that are predominately white. At this stage they were working in black and white in order to concentrate on the relationship between type and image shapes.

7.

These two photographs of Juvelen were provided by the artist for incorporation in the design.

 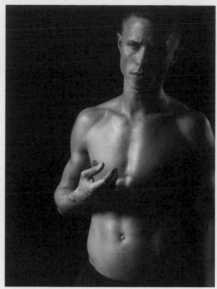

8.

The designers developed and refined the shapes illustration, and included colour, soft shading and highlights using the software program. Juvelen is Swedish for jewel, and this influenced the design, which has reflective surfaces and a jewel-like quality.

9.

Grandpeople experimented further with colour, and with incorporating one of the photographs with a variety of shapes, both in colour and black and white.

10.

These images show the finished typeface, designed specifically for the album and booklet, and the finalized logo design that was incorporated into the finished products.

11.

For the final design, one of the amorphous shapes was combined with the photograph, then cut up and rearranged in a faceted design that resembles a cut precious stone – a jewel.

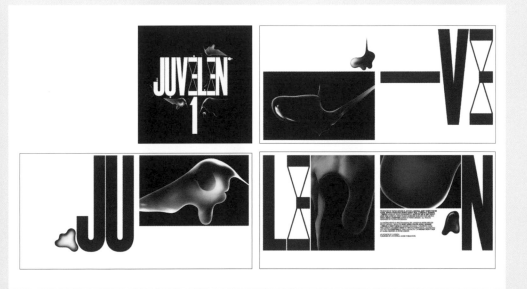

12.

The finished designs for the booklet incorporate the logo, typeface and different developments of the shapes. In terms of composition, the use of regular and irregular shapes gives variety to the different pages of the CD brochure. Where the composition spreads across more than one page, it helps to break up the standard format that is determined by the plastic CD case.

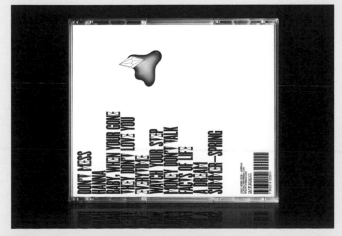

13.

The design for the back of the CD case, using the bespoke typeface and a single shape. It is black on white, which picks up on the white of the title and provides a contrast with the rest of the design, which has a black background.

14.

The final cover design for the CD 'jewel case' incorporates the logo and shapes.

Communication

4

Use of image, by its nature, is communication. The person/people you wish to communicate with, and the message you are trying to convey will dictate, to some extent, the images that you use. All images carry a message of some sort – you cannot use an image without conveying a meaning or opening it up to interpretation.

Opposite: in this series of posters for Harvey Nichols, DDB London have used strong, disturbing images of apparently distressed mannequins to convey the message about the forthcoming sale.

Information
or Persuasion

Visual communication can be split broadly into two categories: information and persuasion. The use of images can be different in each case. Images used in information, for example, help people to understand something, whereas in advertising and propaganda the purpose of the communication is to change the audience's perception and persuade them to buy into a viewpoint or product. This chapter describes how images can be used effectively to entice or challenge the viewer.

Whether you are designing a political poster or a children's book, the design should aim to provoke the reader to decipher the message. This includes directing the viewer or reader to the message, around the message and to an understanding of the meaning of the communication.

 If a poster or other design is seen in company with a number of similar artefacts, all shouting for attention, the result may become just visual noise.

Visual communication is most effective when the audience is not aware they are being persuaded. This also applies when information is communicated in order to provide clarity or enhance the written content of a publication: the design should not make viewers aware of how a message is being conveyed; it should just convey information effectively.

 When deciding on a persuasive image, remember that you are not preaching to the converted. If you were trying to persuade young people to listen to classical music, for example, you would be unlikely to be successful if you chose pictures that reflected a traditional classical style and did not embrace youth culture, its fashions and dynamics.

Josh Gidman has overlayed both signage and unspoken direction indicators, such as the pigeon, to convey the complexity of the urban environment.

This notice board has layers of posters all competing for attention. It is unlikely that any one poster's message will come across loud and clear above the din.

This early map uses images to help the
viewer identify sites and understand the
nature of the places, for example elephants
in India.

❶ The design shown opposite, by Asbjørn
Andvig, is intended to shock. An image
of someone being tortured is laid over the
United States flag, which is associated with
freedom and the rights of the individual. The
designer has used a mixture of printmaking
and distressing techniques to increase the
strength of the image's message.

Directing the Reader to the Message

Conveying a message effectively involves directing the audience to the important areas of the design first, and ensuring they are guided through all areas of the communication. Most design requires the audience to be drawn into the message and one of the ways to draw attention to it is through the use of hierarchy.

Hierarchy

Images can be used in the same way as title, headings and subheadings (as in this book) to guide the reader through a story. This is often done by using a large image to draw the reader in, as in magazines where the front cover usually uses an image of a person looking out at the reader. The main image may represent the content, providing the clue as to the message, or it may be something that is shocking or startling and is used to draw the reader's eye. This trick is used with pull quotes in newspapers and magazines.

'...draw the reader in by shocking them, as the tabloids often do with outrageous headlines...'

Shock tactics

An image that is outrageous or stands out in some other way, stopping the viewer in their tracks, can be achieved by various means such as scale and breaking the flow, as well as issues regarding colour (discussed in Chapter 5).

If you flicked through this book, as people often do with books (often from back to front because this is a natural ergonomic action), you probably stopped briefly at this spread because of the shock value of the image on the right-hand page. This was intentional and is an example of the power images have to stop people in their tracks. ❶

Other ways of using shock tactics to make a reader/viewer stop and look are contrasts in scale – for example, a small tree next to an enormous pigeon – large, empty spaces, rude words, very large or very small type and using inappropriate colour. There is also the obvious use of slightly dubious content, such as sexual innuendo, body parts or culturally taboo subjects.

In a magazine or similar publication, shock can be created by interrupting the rhythm of a series of spreads, in the same way that a musician might create a pause or emphasis by inserting a discordant, different note or, indeed, silence. A simple example in a narrative setting would be a series of spreads in a picture book where the rhythm is created through light, airy images that are interrupted by a dark, night scene.

Such shock tactics are also used in on-screen design. Often a splash or opening page is designed to shock or alarm viewers so that they pause to look at the content rather than moving on to the next web site. Ways of capturing attention are particularly important in web site design as people aren't looking at a magazine or physical object, and therefore they need to be prevented from leaving the site behind. This is similar to flicking through channels on television as opposed to sitting in a cinema as a captive audience.

Similarly, when the audience isn't captive, or is moving, for example when they see an advertisement or hoarding on the side of the road rather than looking at one while standing next to it, it is necessary to do something that makes them absorb the information quickly because usually they don't have the opportunity to study it. Shock tactics are often employed here, such as the use of a strong image or an unexpected element.

When designing a poster, it is useful to know where it is likely to be sited, as shock tactics may be needed for it to be noticed among lots of other posters and information. This is also often the case with internal noticeboards, and applies to smaller items such as the small ads at the back of many magazines and in newspapers.

Be careful when you use shocking images, as something you may consider an innocent joke may be offensive to someone else. You should also take equal opportunity issues, such as those relating to sexism and racism, into consideration.

SINCE 1976, THERE HAVE BEEN 1,099
EXECUTIONS IN THE UNITED STATES

IN 2007, THERE WERE 3,350 PRISONERS
AWAITING EXECUTION IN THE UNITED STATES.

AN EXECUTION, IS TORTURE, INVOLVING

AN ASSAULT ON A HUMAN BEING

Thinking differently

Satire, on its own or combined with humour, may be used
to provoke a response by making people think twice about a
message. Political cartoons are used in this way, particularly
in newspapers and magazines. Their impact is immediate,
but is short-lived as they rely on current affairs, whereas
satire used in advertising may be more subtle and draw on
a wider range of meanings to convey the message, as in
the examples shown on the right.

This image by Ian Pollock takes a satirical
swipe at supermarkets' attempts to follow
an environmental agenda.

For this poster Beth Walker chose an
image that makes the viewer think twice
by relating freedom and pets to fashion.

Claes Oldenburg's sculptures invite the viewer to perceive everyday objects, such as this
light switch, differently: in a new light.

Visual Continuity

Whatever tactics are used to draw the viewer into the message, you need to guide them through the information by using visual continuity. This is where aspects of the design obviously relate, and belong, to each other. This may be achieved by various means, such as the same margin measurements throughout a publication, similar typefaces and chapter openings, the use of specific colours or the positioning of page numbers and headers and footers. These devices can be applied to an entire publication or to sections of a book, newspaper or magazine.

When you are designing a publication, visual continuity helps to reinforce its identity but, if followed slavishly, it may become boring. An example would be a magazine where one style of layout, or the same grid, was used for all pages. The magazine's identity would be clear, but the reader would probably soon lose interest. As we saw in Chapter 2, a grid that is used similarly throughout a publication can make it look staid and may even result in the reader giving up.

Rhythm and repetition

Rhythm and repetition are useful in providing continuity as people naturally respond to them – when listening to music they tap their feet or fingers – and images, repeated or slightly altered, can be used to draw the audience in.

However, rhythm and repetition are not necessarily the same. Repetition does what it says, that is, it repeats a phrase or action, whereas rhythm may be repetitious but can also be made up of quite complex structures where the repetition is not apparent. Both can be used to create visual continuity but repetition, as when all the pages in a publication have the same underlying grid, can be easy to spot whereas rhythm may be more subtle. An example would be where there are variations in the underlying grid, such as two- and three-column versions with the same margins and typeface.

Although repetition is useful it should be used with caution and a *less is more* approach should be applied. As mentioned earlier, repeated use of the same devices can lead to boredom and disengagement on the reader's part. A magazine in which the images were the same size and in the same position on every page could be seen as tedious, and would not be as inviting as one where there was a variety of sizes and positions used.

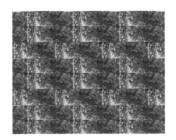 

Mary Davis has used a tight crop from a larger image to create an abstract rhythmic pattern. The strong use of horizontal strips of various widths that contrast with the vertical strokes is reminiscent of musical staves.

These sugar pigs look effective repeated side by side whereas the impact would be lost if only one pig was shown.

Mnemonics

Another way of providing continuity is by using visual mnemonics (an obscure term for a simple concept). Traditionally, a mnemonic is a rhyme to help with memorizing something, such as Every Good Boy Deserves a Football for the notes on the musical stave or Naughty Elephants Squirt Water for the points of the compass. In the same way, images can act as memory joggers; an image of an elephant, for example, might suggest something you should remember. This concept is similar to that of ideograms, discussed in the introduction to this book. A pictogram can be used consistently as a mnemonic throughout a magazine or web site to remind readers or viewers of the identity of the publication or site.

 When using visual mnemonics, be aware that some images have multiple meanings: as well as acting as a reminder, an image of an elephant may also suggest something large, cumbersome, endangered, etc.

Mnemonics can help to ensure a design is memorable, either because they are good to look at or because they are controversial or ugly. This could be achieved not only by the image itself, but also by the use of colour or text in combination with the image. The relationship between the different components of a design can change the meaning of the communication.

Phillip Skinner's design for a web site uses
the familiar pictogram of a person running
to reinforce the site's title: lastminute.com.

Visual and Verbal Synergy

Visual and verbal synergy can help the reader/audience to understand a communication as well as aiding visual continuity by linking elements of the content. This synergy is achieved when the images used are in harmony with the written content. The reader is guided by the use of images and text that work together, supporting the communication. Viewers usually understand images more quickly than they understand text and therefore images often replace text in order to get a message across more directly and speedily – for example, in information graphics. Alternatively, an image may not entirely replace the text but may support it or provide extra information, or the text itself may be viewed as an object or image in its own right.

When images are in harmony with both the written content and the typography, a design achieves visual and verbal synergy. The interaction between word and picture dictates how the viewer interprets the message. ❶

Visual and verbal synergy is effective in directing the audience but, as with harmony and discord, discussed in Chapter 3, an image that appears to contradict the text may also help to convey meaning. However, this may rely on the audience understanding the contextual disharmony. An example would be a poster persuading people not to smoke, in which the image shows a glamorous person but the words refer to coughing, bad breath, smelly clothes, lung cancer and other issues related to the downsides of smoking. There are some situations where this kind of more subtle approach would be totally unsuitable, for instance, when the communication has to be seen and understood very quickly. An example of this would be a sign warning people that there is a danger of being eaten. ❷

❶ Jason Munn's design demonstrates how an image can be linked to a title or heading.

❷ This warning sign prioritizes the visual part of the image, using the words as supplementary information, as images are usually understood faster than words.

Pictures replacing text

The saying 'A picture is worth a thousand words' is worth remembering, as an image can quite often replace words. This is particularly useful in advertising and web design where reading can be difficult. A poster on the side of a taxi, for example, often flashes by the viewer and doesn't give them time to read the text. A poster inside a taxi, however, might be more text-based because the audience is captive and stationary.

Another instance where an image replaces text is the rebus, which is often used as a device to attract attention and is not always easily understood at first glance. This approach falls into the more subtle method of persuasion, where a puzzle or oddity attracts the viewer and they pause to decipher the message. The most common form of rebus is when words are replaced with pictograms; an example is an image of a bee replacing the word 'be' or the letter B. Rebuses are used to amuse people or puzzle them, or to communicate a joke, and are often seen in children's books. Texting, where numbers and letters are used to shorten the volume of words, is based on similar principles. An example is 'To be or not to be…' which in text speak would be translated as '2 B or not 2 B'. ❶

Pictures supplementing text

It is not just children who like images with their words. In textbooks, images such as technical diagrams or illustrations provide additional detail or contextualizing information. Pictures can also bring a story to life by developing characters or scenes or by putting the story into a historical or contemporary context, although this may not always work – giving form to imaginary places and figures can be at odds with the reader's interpretation of the text. We have all been disappointed with a film's depiction of a favourite book or story. ❷

Some forms of narrative rely heavily on images to deliver the story; graphic novels and comic books, for example, use pictures to replace words in order to get their message across quickly without the reader having to make too much effort. Normally, this requires the imagery and text to be developed simultaneously as they are interdependent; this way of working also helps to avoid misinterpretations. The text is often integrated with the images and may even become an image in itself, as in explosions in comics which often have words such as BAM! in large hand-lettering.

Cartoon by Dave Colton integrating text with image to convey the action of an explosion.

❶ This rebus uses images to replace words for the quotation from *Hamlet* 'To be or not to be…'

❷ In this image Lester Meachem has developed the character of the witch from *Hansel and Gretel* into a warty, biscuit-loving old crone.

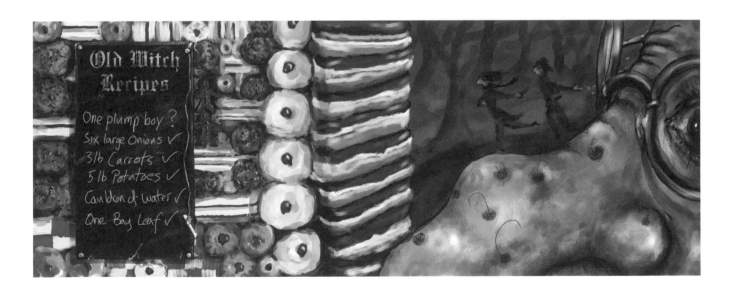

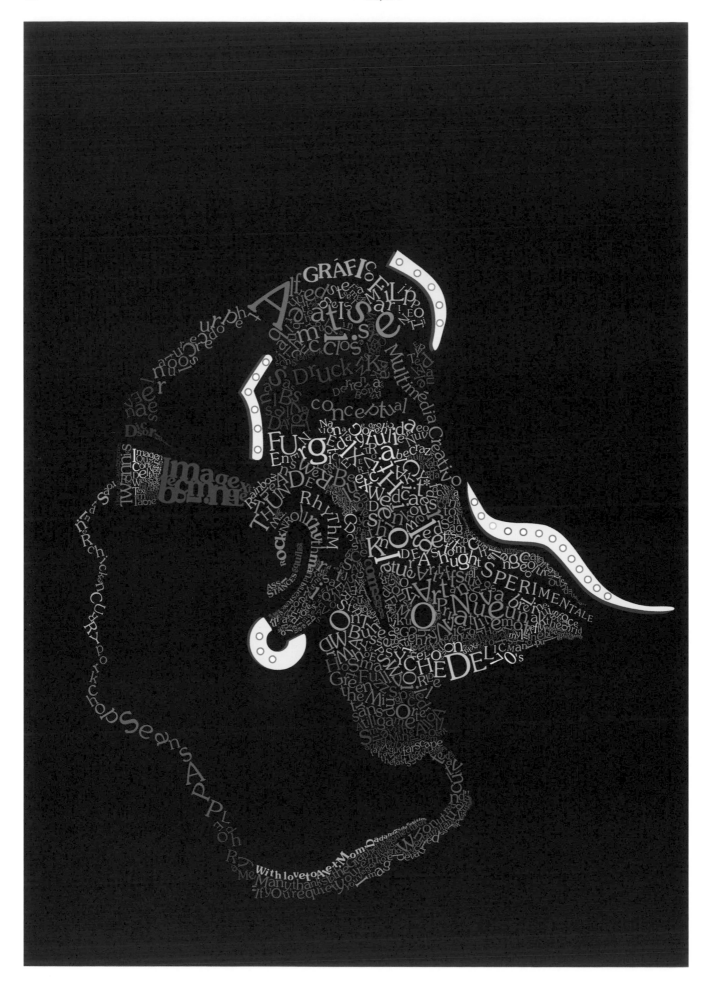

Opposite: in Sean Bird's image words
have been used as a drawing device; they
retain the flowing curves of brushstrokes
but, at the same time, remain legible.

Text becoming image

When text is identified as an image it can be quickly interpreted and aids communication. Letterforms or bodies of text may be used as objects/images in their own right or may form part of an image. The most obvious use of this is for logotypes, such as the Volkswagen (VW) logo which has become identified as an image rather than text. Once established, such logotypes are easily identified with the company or brand concerned and are often used to associate it to positive aspects of life, or events such as football teams or racing cars. In some instances, words may completely replace imagery in that they are transformed into images. Another example is where words are used as part of the pictorial content, just as drawn marks or shapes can be used to form the image.

Whether or not an image is made from text, it can be used to convey a variety of meanings which may be complex and varied.

In this context RADIO works as a recognizable symbol even though the audience may not be familiar with the literal translation of the word.

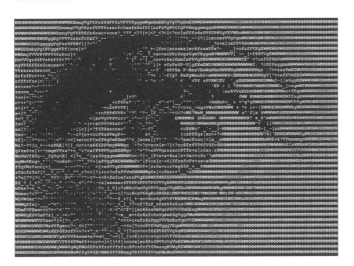

Letters and numbers have been used to recreate the different tones in this image of an eye.

This logo is identified with the Ban the Bomb movement.

Opposite: Amirali Ghasemi's use of quickly
drawn shapes contrasts well with the
technical illustrations and gives the design
a lively appearance which would probably
be difficult with just technical drawings.

Transmitting Meanings

Meaning can be transmitted in various ways, some of which are
very sophisticated. It is important to understand the meanings
associated with any images used in a design to ensure that the
message is transmitted in the way it was intended. In the same
way that some words have different meanings depending on
the context – 'fine' can be used to describe the details in a work
of art or the state of the weather – images can be understood
in different ways depending on the context in which they are
used. Style may also affect meaning: a lively sketch could
convey immediacy and spontaneity (on the other hand, it could
make a design look unfinished).

Some companies exist purely to support the need for
meaning to be communicated effectively; for example, some
advertising agencies employ psychologists to help them develop
the meanings behind their messages. Sometimes, multiple
meanings are incorporated into a design; some of these may
be complex, underpinning messages which the audience is
not necessarily aware of, but which will reach them anyway.

When communicating, people often use comparison as a
way of clarifying what they mean. The best comparisons are
those that are recognized across different cultures and are part of
everyday life: for example, walking through a muddy field would
be a comparison with something that is difficult to achieve.

Images can be used to communicate an idea, like the dove
with an olive branch, which is used as a symbol for peace.
A combination of symbols can convey a difficult message, as
in the example shown on page 112 where the two symbols
represent meanings that work against each other. The overall
message is one of no entry, but the closed zip offers the
possibility of an opening, and the qualifying statement is that
you don't get in unless you are good.

The example shown on page 111 could be seen as the use
of positive and negative symbols. The combination of symbols
with positive and negative meanings and associations can help
to communicate a complicated message and/or make the
viewer think about the message.

Both these images include apples but the intended meanings are quite different. The
happy child about to bite into an apple seems to convey youth, health and happiness
whereas the other image seems to play on the apple's association with temptation.

In the first design Aarefa Tayabji uses the images to attract an audience to something they
will enjoy (top) whereas the other designer uses similar silhouetted images to convey a
quite different message about the relationship between music and business (bottom).

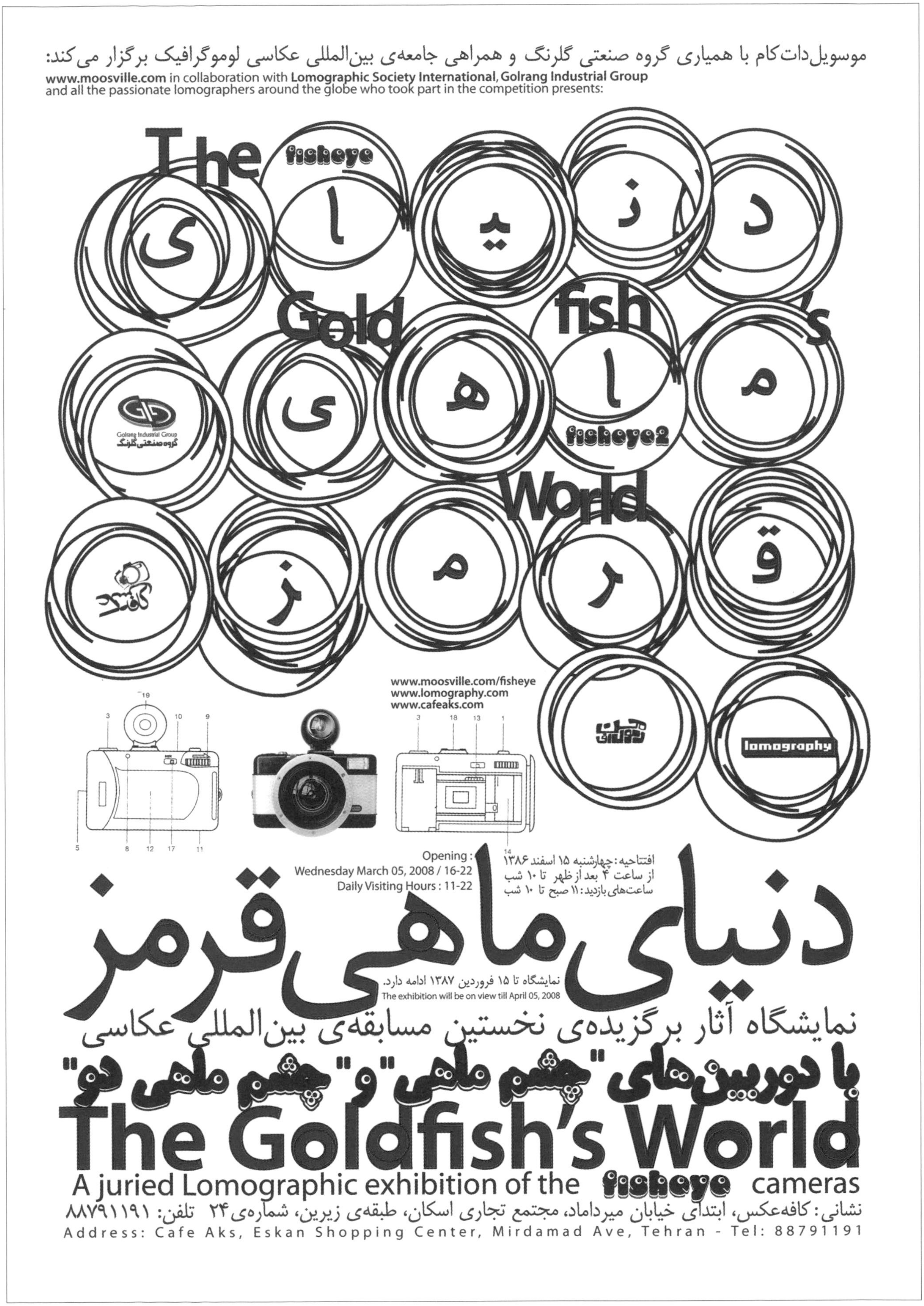
موسویل‌دات‌کام با همیاری گروه صنعتی گلرنگ و همراهی جامعه‌ی بین‌المللی عکاسی لوموگرافیک برگزار می‌کند:
www.moosville.com in collaboration with Lomographic Society International, Golrang Industrial Group
and all the passionate lomographers around the globe who took part in the competition presents:
The
fisheye
Gold
fish
's
fisheye2
World
Golrang Industrial Group
گروه صنعتی گلرنگ
lomography
www.moosville.com/fisheye
www.lomography.com
www.cafeaks.com
Opening :
Wednesday March 05, 2008 / 16-22
Daily Visiting Hours : 11-22
افتتاحیه: چهارشنبه ۱۵ اسفند ۱۳۸۶
از ساعت ۴ بعد از ظهر تا ۱۰ شب
ساعت‌های بازدید: ۱۱ صبح تا ۱۰ شب
دنیای ماهی قرمز
نمایشگاه تا ۱۵ فروردین ۱۳۸۷ ادامه دارد.
The exhibition will be on view till April 05, 2008
نمایشگاه آثار برگزیده‌ی نخستین مسابقه‌ی بین‌المللی عکاسی
با دوربین‌های "چشم ماهی" و "چشم ماهی دو"
The Goldfish's World
A juried Lomographic exhibition of the fisheye cameras
نشانی: کافه‌عکس، ابتدای خیابان میرداماد، مجتمع تجاری اسکان، طبقه‌ی زیرین، شماره‌ی ۲۴ تلفن: ۸۸۷۹۱۱۹۱
Address: Cafe Aks, Eskan Shopping Center, Mirdamad Ave, Tehran - Tel: 88791191

Below: this illustration by Jon Rhodes uses a combination of a light butterfly with a solid, utilitarian tool. The underpinning message is about the mechanics behind much that we perceive as natural and beautiful in today's world.

Opposite: there are three messages in the image by Jason Munn: war, peace and freedom. War is symbolized by the shape of a bomb and peace by the dove; the more complex, but understandable, use of the open cage with the dove flying out of it represents freedom. If the door of the cage were closed, or if the bomb were solid rather than made of wire, the meaning would be different as it could indicate that the solid bomb was a threat to the dove or, if the door were closed, that the dove had no influence over it: peace would not overcome war.

TED LEO + PHARMACISTS

GEORGIE JAMES | SO MANY DYNAMOS | PONY COME LATELY

MARCH 2, 2007 | GREAT AMERICAN MUSIC HALL | NOISE POP 15

Juxtaposition of symbols may change
meaning, as in this image by Zane Manasco
where the zip conveys opening and the
circle with a diagonal line is a commonly
used symbol for forbidden or no entry.

Activity

Two positives can make a negative. Find pictures of twenty objects, ten of which you feel have positive connotations and ten that have negative ones. Try juxtaposing the images to see how they can affect each other's meaning.

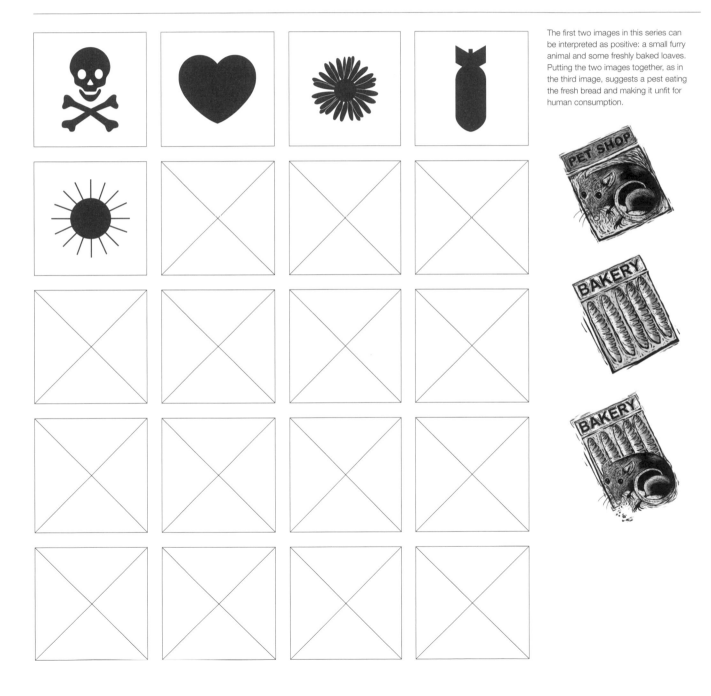

The first two images in this series can be interpreted as positive: a small furry animal and some freshly baked loaves. Putting the two images together, as in the third image, suggests a pest eating the fresh bread and making it unfit for human consumption.

1 Each of these posters by Phillip Skinner, which are intended to be viewed on the move, conveys a small amount of information, which builds into a single message by the time the viewer has reached the bottom of the escalator.

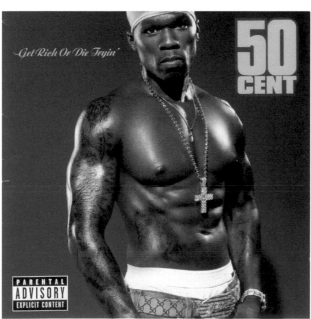

Pictures of the performers are clues to the contents of both of these CDs. They would mean very little to someone not familiar with the particular styles of music.

Communication in context

The use of similar or contradictory symbols is complex and suited only to particular situations, and audiences who have knowledge of the subject or issues involved. This is often the case with album or specialist magazine covers. Not everyone belongs to a club or group, and communication that relies on an understanding of specific interests will not work for most people.

When considering communication, it is usually best to make a design as simple as possible. This is becoming increasingly important as our lives get busier and we are bombarded by more and more information. For instance, posters are seen everywhere, and advertisements and billboards line major roads and motorways. This means the message has to be conveyed at a glance and cannot be obscured.

In an environment where there is a captive audience, such as on an underground escalator, it is possible to use multiple images which, although obscure individually, collectively convey meaning. ❶

Communication style

It is necessary to consider style as well as context when considering how to communicate the meaning associated with a design. If the message is serious, a formal, spartan approach may convey the meaning more effectively than a fussy flamboyant style. However, style is largely determined by the designer and is not necessarily influenced by the content: some designers have easily recognized styles which they apply to a variety of communications. Jean-Benoît Lévy has a particular way of using type and images, which makes much of his work recognizable even though the content of his designs varies and they are directed at different audiences (as seen over the page).

Below: these two pieces of work by Jean-Benoît Lévy have a consistent style even though they were designed for different purposes.

Opposite: this poster for Nike has a lively feel, using overlapping images to convey the high levels of activity associated with the brand.

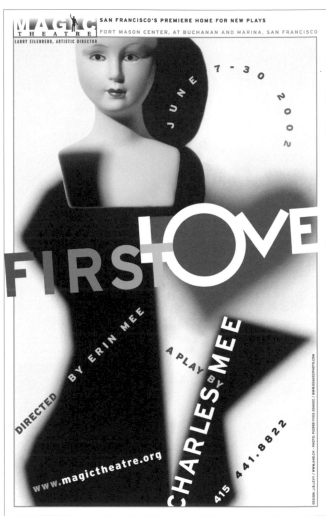

Case Study
Photophilliac, Zane Manasco, Gibraltar

1.

To collect examples of found text, Zane took photographs of walls in Gibraltar where posters had been applied on top of other posters. Over time, some of the images and text had become fragmented as a result of various layers being superimposed and then torn, weathered or scratched away.

To explore his interest in the use of text as a visual rather than verbal form of communication, Zane Manasco designs and produces his own magazine *Photophilliac*, an experimental magazine with a limited print run (1,000 copies). He uses found text and images that have been distressed and overlaid with unrelated text and images, and explores communication through the layering of visual and textual material. Because Zane has total editorial control, he can allow the imagery to develop organically, with the final images emerging from the found sources. They continually react with each other in the way a conversation or dialogue is constructed, and gradually develop and coalesce into a design solution.

2.

For the cover of the magazine, Zane started with a series of sketches that looked at ways in which the photographs could be combined with his own text. By distressing the text and images to the point of abstraction, he strained the boundaries of legibility in favour of aesthetics and composition. In this way, he brought the text and images closer together. He states that his aim was to achieve visual and verbal synergy within the final pieces by breaking up the legibility of both the text and images to the point at which they become just compositional shapes and colours within the design. The design itself has become abstracted and the message is not obvious or straightforward.

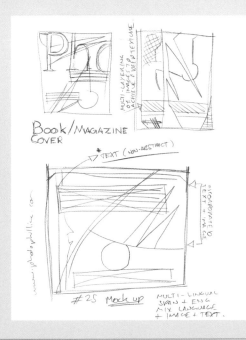

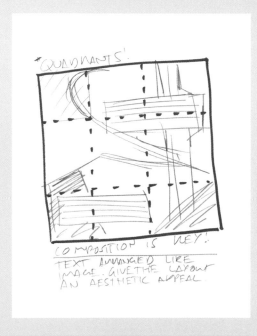

3.

The designer combined aspects of the found images to produce a single image for the cover. He chose this use of text and images because he considered that it provided the most visual impact to draw the viewer in, even though the message itself has become ambiguous.

4.

Originally, Zane intended that the image should stand alone, with the title and explanatory text hidden or disguised within it. This was an experimental approach to communication that would rely on a sophisticated audience to decipher it. However, after exploring the extent to which he could abstract the image and text, he decided he had gone too far, in that his message was being lost, and introduced the title and subheading of the publication in order to provide clarity while retaining an ambiguous quality.

5.

After adding the title, Zane experimented with transparency of text. His reasoning was that he did not want the title and subhead to dominate the composition; rather, he wanted them to become part of the underlying image creating a more balanced relationship between the text and image. He was concerned that he had taken the design and composition too far in the opposite direction, towards the obvious, with a strong reliance on text for communication.

6.

Zane started by subsuming the text into the image, so that it almost became lost, but then changed his mind and made the text much more dominant because of the need to communicate essential information. In his words, he 'wanted to explore the power/function/form of text within an image to the point of it taking over…'

After producing the integrated image, he needed to incorporate further information, including the web address, ensuring that this did not detract from the visual communication and impact.

Colour

5

Although there are excellent examples of design in black and white, colour can make a difference to the way a message is communicated. This chapter discusses how colour can affect meaning, the various ways in which it can be used and the effects that can be achieved with it.

Colour is usually categorized by hue, which is colour in its pure form. The primary and secondary colours on the colour wheel are hues. The brightness of a colour refers to how dark or light it is, so if white is added to a hue it will be brighter (a tint) whereas adding black will make a colour darker (a shade). The saturation of a colour refers to how pure the hue is so, a pure hue is fully saturated. It is useful to be familiar with colour terminology as it ensures you will be able to communicate your design ideas and intentions clearly. For example, when using the full range of colours available in a design for print, if you use the term 'full colour' the printer will be familiar with the effect you intend to achieve.

Opposite: Inksurge have used flat areas of colour overlaid with simple pattern in some areas of the illustration. The dark colour provides strong outlines on the blues and greens and the red has been used for accent.

These examples by Bunch Design
demonstrate the effect produced by
using different saturations of one colour.

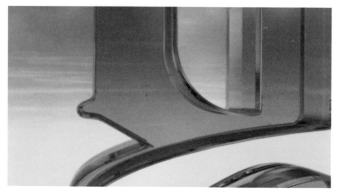

Using Colour in Print

When designing for print it is useful to understand the way colour is reproduced and the terminology associated with this. As well as full colour, there are colour-matching systems, which are used to match specific colours, and spot colour which is usually used for emphasis on an otherwise single-colour print.

Full colour

Full colour refers to reproducing a full range of colours as near as possible to the original, using four printing-process colours. If you wanted to reproduce a coloured photograph of a bowl of fruit for a magazine article, the full-colour printing process will get as close as possible to the original image.

Various types of colour mode are available digitally, such as lab colour, indexed colour and multichannel, but the one that is used most frequently is RGB, which stands for red green blue, the three colours that make up the digital colour range. However, when designing for print the options are more restricted. Currently, much full-colour print is made up from the four-colour process CMYK, which has its origins in the offset lithography system which used four screens made up of dots (like a newspaper image magnified), each of which printed a single colour – cyan (C), magenta (M), yellow (Y) or black (K) – to produce a full-colour image. Most colours can be obtained using the CMYK process, but sometimes it is not possible to reproduce certain ones accurately; where this is the case, extra colours can be added using specially mixed inks. Such colours are found in charts or swatches produced for colour-matching systems. This does not apply when designing on screen, as digital platforms provide the full range of colours available.

This leads to another issue: when designing on a computer, remember that the colour you see on screen (which is light-emitting) will not look the same when it is printed (light-reflective). One way around this is to calibrate your monitor with your inkjet or laser printer. However, usually this will apply only to the printer you use for personal proofing and not to a commercial one. The normal solution is to get the printing house to supply a proof that you can check for colour accuracy.

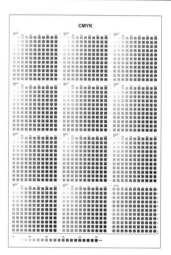

The chart shows colours produced by various combinations of CMYK. This is useful if you are trying to match a particular colour within the four-colour process.

A swatch of colours used for matching specific colours following, for example, the Pantone® Matching System.

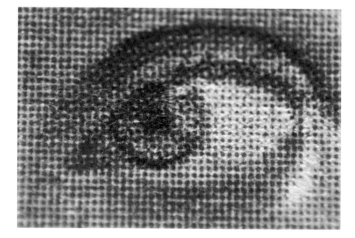

This shows a close-up of the roseate of dots that make up the CMYK printing process, using a separate screen for each of the four colours. When looked at close-up like this they are obvious, but when seen in print the individual dots cannot be seen and the colour mixes optically to make the full colour range.

Colour-matching systems

The Pantone® Matching System (PMS) and similar systems allow accurate colour reproduction within printing processes. Although they can be used for single-colour prints, they are often used to match a particular colour that is difficult to obtain using the CMYK process colours. For example, certain yellows can be difficult to reproduce accurately. Matching a specific colour may be overlooked if only a small area of a larger image is involved, but can be very important if a company's logo is being reproduced as part of a full-colour print or if the image – a medical or botanical illustration, for example – requires accurate colour. Specific colours can be matched using the Pantone colour guides. PMS colours can also be used as specially applied spot colours.

As is clear from magazines and many newspapers, full-colour printing is cheap and readily available. However, the quality of reproduction may vary as it relies heavily on the stock used (stock is discussed more fully in Chapter 7) and it is worth asking the printer's advice or looking at samples of print on different stock.

Single- or two-colour printing

Colour printing provides complete information but can sometimes obscure content. For example black-and-white images are usually clear and strong as the tones provide the information whereas colour images can bombard the viewer with too much information and tonal values may be obscured, with backgrounds and foregrounds becoming one. Single- or two-colour printing can be effective in providing contrast, both in the images and in variations from what has become the accepted norm in full-colour printing.

The use of one colour is referred to as single-colour printing. Although this may often be black on white, any single colour can be used, and could be reproduced, to great effect, on stock – the paper or other material on which the image is printed – of a colour other than white. When specifying colours other than full colour for print, the number of colours is referred to. So, red and black would be two colour and, as before, the stock would not need to be white.

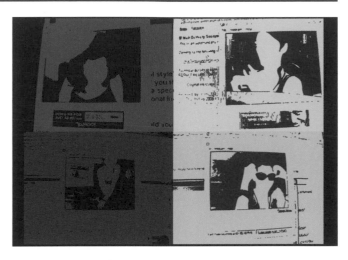

In this web design, Amirali Ghasemi has used black on a single colour for each section which provides contrast and interest, making the pages stand out.

This design by Sean Bird, produced as part of a student project and not taken to production stage, uses two colours on white paper to produce a strong design, dominated by the image.

The mood of Ludovic Balland's poster is enhanced by the use of a light blue stock as the background to a strong combination of black image and text, which provides contrast and clarity.

Bunch Design have used a three-colour combination in this design for themed flyers and posters.

Top: in 'There is no wave without wind'
Selina Pan has used spot colour to pick
out the leaping, typographically
constructed fish. The red colour
emphasizes the shape of the fish against
the more delicate background of white
space, and waves illustrated in grey fluid
text. This delicate approach demonstrates
a subtle use of spot colour.

Bottom: spot colour in this advertisement
has been used to good effect –
highlighting the important features: the
iPod logo and the iPod itself.

Spot colour

'Spot colour' refers to the use of one extra colour on a single-colour print – normally a small patch that highlights a specific area. The technique is not just used in print: in many films, such as *The Red Balloon* and *Schindler's List*, spot colour was used to draw attention to an item or person. Although spot colour originated from the need to use colour economically when full colour was expensive, it is now more often used in the way italics, bold and underlining are used in text – for emphasis. The choice of spot colour can underline the communication. For example, pink is usually associated with feminine, girlish, delicate things whereas red, in most Western societies, is symbolic of war.

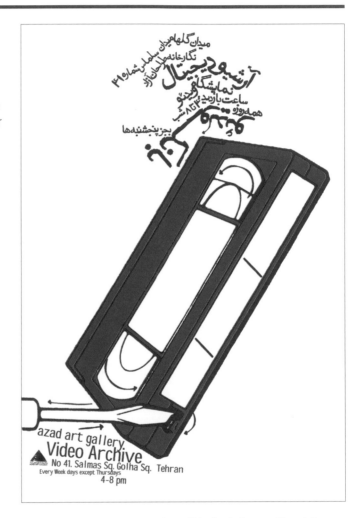

Amirali Ghasemi has used a red spot colour to fill the flat plastic areas of the main image and make them solid, whereas the text and other parts of the design remain as line. This provides contrast as well as drawing attention to the main image, which represents the topic of video archive.

❶ Chris Bolton has used a monochrome image in the design shown opposite to connect the image with the text.

Greyscale

Greyscale refers to an image that is made up of tonal variations: shades of grey, together with black and white. It is also called monochrome, and any colour can be used with white. Greyscale images allow the eye to see tonal ranges which are often obscured or lost in a full-colour image. An image of a furry animal will look softer if there is less contrast and the tonal values are close to each other, while an image of a chrome car bumper looks clearer and harder with a sharp contrast of tones.

The photograph used in this design uses a soft tonal range appropriate to the subject matter. The design, by Ravenshaw Studios, was a winner of a Robert Horne Shout award.

This series of images shows the effect achieved by using duotones or tritones on a monochrome photograph.

Strong contrast between tones is appropriate for this image of reflective metallic surfaces on a building.

A monochrome image is made up from the different tones of a single colour. This does not necessarily mean black on white; it could be orange on white or orange on a yellow paper. ❶

Duotone and tritone

A duotone is a tonal image printed in black and one other colour, which adds a coloured tint to a black-and-white image. It can produce a richer looking image, adding depth and emphasis, and heightening the tonal differences in a monochrome image, depending on the original image and the colour, and can be used to draw the viewer's attention to the image. Tritones are produced using black and two other colours. You can experiment with the depth of tone in different colours to achieve subtle or dramatic effects.

Snug
as a bug
in a rug

Goldlog

❶ In the design shown opposite, Karl Martin Saetren has used a subtle combination of analogous colours to convey a feeling of harmony.

Colour Relationships

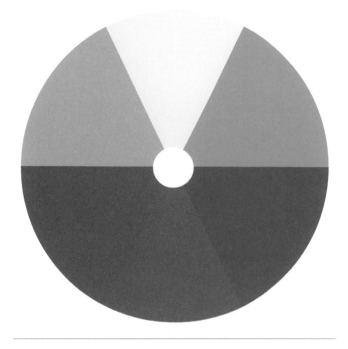

This distinctive design by Adam Rix uses complementary opposites on black to make a strong statement and attract the viewer.

When using colour to create an effect or mood, it is useful to be aware of colour relationships and the effect colours can have on each other. The colour wheel, above, shows how different colours relate to each other depending on where they are positioned within the wheel.

As discussed earlier, hues are pure colours and, on the colour wheel, they are seen as red, blue and yellow (primary colours) and orange, green and purple (secondary colours). Tertiary colours such as turquoise sit between primary and secondary colours on the colour wheel. Other colours are achieved by mixing colours from different areas of the wheel and their related tints and shades. See Further Reading for more information about colour and colour mixing.

Colours on the wheel are described as being complementary opposites or analogous, depending on where they are positioned. Combinations of colours within these two groups, as well as discordant, dominant and accent colours, can be used to create different effects.

Complementary opposites

By complementary colours, we mean colours that are opposite each other on the colour wheel, such as orange and blue. They bounce off and enhance each other. Orange placed next to blue makes the blue appear stronger, and more blue. If someone wears an orange tie on a blue shirt there is a visual vibration where the two colours meet; this can be used effectively to draw attention to elements in a design.

A colour can be affected by background or adjacent colours. If a yellow package is placed on a bright blue background it may appear slightly green; on a red background it may look more orange.

 Care needs to be taken when using complementary opposites as they can cause unintended optical illusions, which can be distracting, irritating or disturbing.

Analogous colours

Analogous colours are those that sit close to each other on the colour wheel, like blue and violet. Such colours are easy on the eye and work well together; they are harmonious. Harmonious colours are easier to work with as they go together naturally and can help a design to appear safe, tranquil and tasteful. **❶**

Chris Bolton uses harmonious colours to
convey the mood of the music packaged.

AEROPLANE

PACIFIC AIR RACE

PACIFIC AIR RACE
DUBCLUB MIX

ABOVE THE CLOUDS

Discordant colours

Discordant colours are combinations of colours that are used at a strength that is not normally associated with them, such as light purple (lilac) with dark yellow (ochre). They do not necessarily differ as markedly as complementary opposites, but they can jar the eye and make an element in a design stand out.

 The saying goes 'all is yellow to the jaundiced eye'. Some colours may appear bright and cheerful to you but could be seen in another way by someone else; especially if they are colour blind.

Gradient

Another way of combining colours, usually available in software, is gradient, where one colour gradually changes to another one within a defined space, such as a box or even across a whole page. Gradients can be very useful but can also appear rather crude: because they are easily achievable digitally, they have been overused. ❶

The dark orange and lighter blue produce a discordant effect in this design by Beth Walker.

Grandpeople's design uses gradient to produce a soft effect for the title 'Love'.

This design by Ed Fella uses discord to create an exceptionally strong poster.

1 In this package design Phillip Skinner has used a gradient on the logo which is made up from the two colours used in the images.

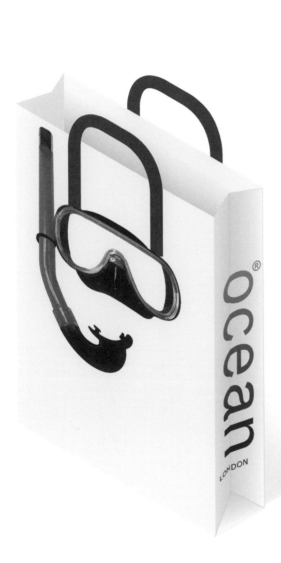

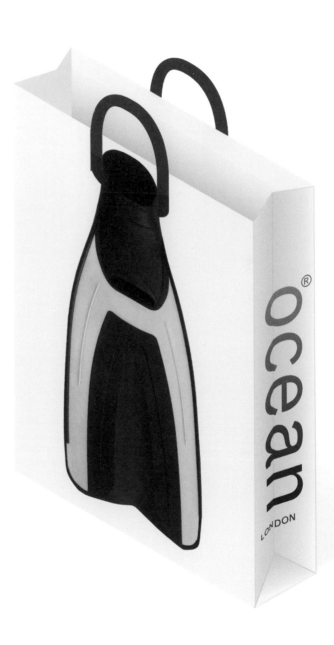

Activity

If you aren't confident about combining or using colours, it's worth collecting successful, or even unsuccessful, examples of colour combinations. These could be taken from a section of a painting, photograph or fabric. Alternatively, you can make your own samples of colour combinations by cutting out pieces of coloured paper (for example, from magazines) and experimenting with different combinations, in twos and threes, to see how the colours work together. You can also experiment like this using software such as Illustrator which provides multiple combinations of colours that technically work well together.

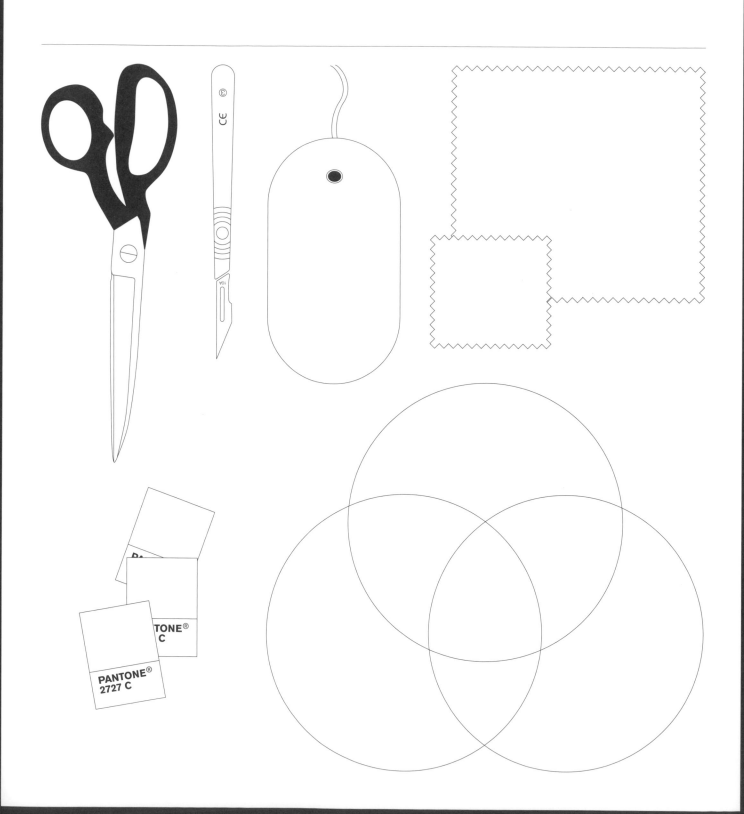

Dominant and accent colours

When colours are put together, one of them is often dominant. This is the colour that will attract the eye, and the weaker colours will complement or contrast with it. A dominant colour is often used as an 'accent colour'. This use of colour is often seen in interior designs where a colour scheme relies principally on two or three subtle shades and a strong colour is used in small doses to add vibrancy and interest. ❶

Accent colours usually work well when they are used in small quantities. In the same way that placing a small object in an otherwise empty space can be very effective by providing emphasis, a bright area of orange, for example, can be very effective in a cream room. This is similar to the use of spot colour.

A trick in magazine design is to use a colour from an image in headings or other graphic items. This has become more prevalent as software makes it easier to isolate and identify colours. Using accent colours in this way can create harmony in a composition. ❷

❶ Elena Proskurova has used blue as an accent colour in picking out the eyes and other areas of the design to make them stand out from the monochrome image.

❷ The designers, Attak, have selected a colour from the image and used it in the title and some of the text, bringing a sense of unity to the design.

❶ In the design shown opposite Luca de Salvia has used red on the fingers in the main image to indicate the warmth associated with massage.

Colour Associations

Accent colours can also be used to associate an image with an activity or organization, as in Gareth Tsang's image of football fans, right. Everyone is familiar with combinations of colours having associations with teams, but there are many other colour combinations that have significance; yellow and black indicating a warning, and red and green for stop and go are examples.

Individual colours have associations but these may differ depending on cultures and beliefs. Red is often interpreted as a warning in the Western world whereas in China it is regarded as extremely lucky. There are certain areas of design, such as food packaging, where some colours are inappropriate. For instance, green would not be suitable for meat packaging as it may have connotations of mould. However, it would be appropriate for packaging for frozen vegetables, not only because many vegetables are green but also because of the colour's association with growth and freshness. ❶

How a designer interprets colour can be influenced by his or her own preferences or favourite colours. This is not necessarily a bad thing as an individual approach to the use of a colour, or unusual combination of colours, can make a design distinctive.

Gareth Tsang has used a limited and specific colour combination related to a particular football team.

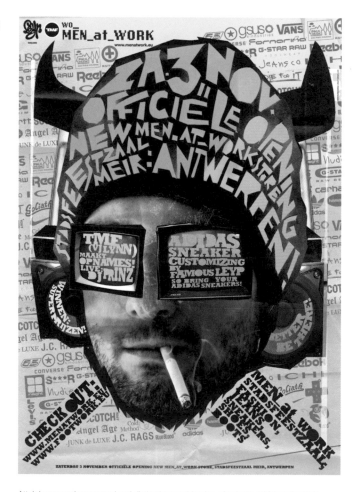

Attak have used an unusual and distinctive combination of colours, which makes this design stand out.

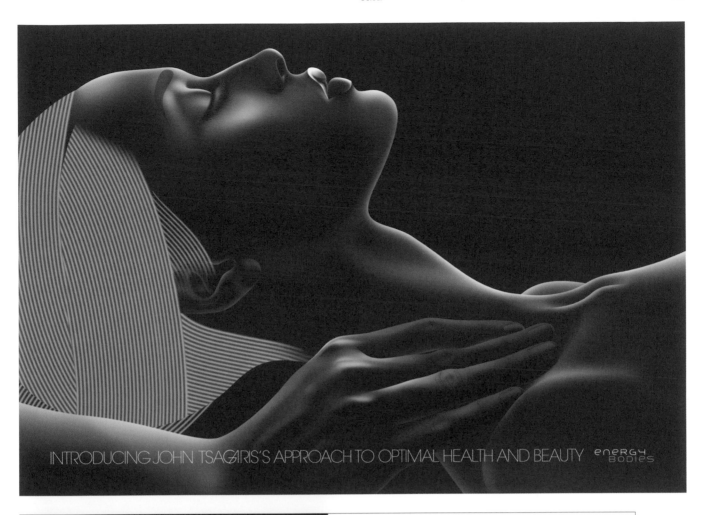

INTRODUCING JOHN TSAGARIS'S APPROACH TO OPTIMAL HEALTH AND BEAUTY   eneRGY BODIES

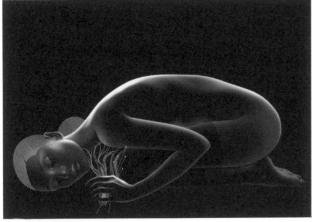

HE MU

The treatment that John Tsagaris calls He Mu (in Chinese this means Harmony) combines traditional Chinese medical applications with aspects of Western medical views. It includes dynamic Zen Shiatsu, traditional acupuncture, oriental healing and Chinese herbal medicine. In addition, he offers advice on diet and lifestyle, as a part of his holistic approach.

John Tsagaris starts his treatments with shiatsu bodywork that facilitates muscular

and energy release and it operates as a tuning and diagnostic tool. This way he stimulates the regulatory systems of the body to give to the patient a sense of profound relaxation and introduces the acupuncture treatment and healing intervention. Acupuncture enables the body's energy network meridians, to transmit information between the brain and the body, to restore or maintain the balance of the body and mind.
Chinese herbal medicine is often used as a

part of John Tsagaris treatments in a form of a unique prescription of Chinese herbs (GM and sulphur-free and approved by UK regulations) or a milder prepared herbal medicine in order to address individual health concerns.
John Tsagaris has studied many different healing techniques, from West and East. Throughout the treatment, the constant energy flow of Reiki and Oriental healing techniques enhance the body's ability to heal itself.

"THOSE WHO SEE HIM RAVE ABOUT HOW GOOD HE MAKES THEM FEEL" MARTIZA BASWAR/ AMIES BEST TREATMENTS

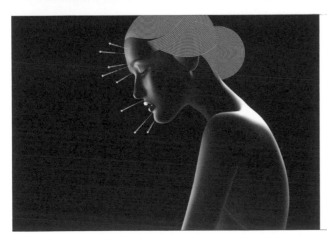

BEAUTY ACUPUNCTURE

Beauty acupuncture stimulates the body's ability to regenerate itself by accelerating anti-inflammatory activity and removing accumulative toxins from the skin. Energy and blood flow throughout the facial skin and muscles is stimulated by the application of needles to key points and areas on the face, head and body. Acupuncture prevents the formation of wrinkles, minimizes the appearance of fine lines and improves

the processes through which the skin regulates its quality and its appearance.

John Tsagaris's treatment, a combination of facial shiatsu, reflexology and acupuncture techniques, increases the flow of oxygen and nutrients to the face in order to reduce visible signs of aging bringing a youthful glow to the face. Collagen production is increased and skin fibres are strengthened.

facial muscles plumped and puffiness reduced around the eyes.

The "whole body" facial beauty acupuncture treatment is an exclusive skin rejuvenating method that unlocks not only the ability of the face to reflect a healthier and younger appearance but also addresses internal causes of premature ageing.

"ONE OF THE BEST NATURAL ALTERNATIVES TO BOTOX" GRAZIA

Brand identity

Combinations of colours, or individual colours, can be used in brand identity. Colour in packaging can affect the customer's perception of a product. The same applies to colour in the formation of a brand identity. Carefully used, it will support the emotional associations that the brand wishes to represent; red, for example, has emotional connotations with heat and passion, and therefore would be appropriate for a hot spicy product or a flamenco dance troupe.

However, colour can be overused in brand identity, and can also convey the wrong signals if the use of a particular colour is not thought through carefully in terms of different cultural associations. This is particularly important in the light of international trade and the use of the Internet for marketing and advertising, where a site may be available across the world.

Many companies and institutions have strict guidelines and policies related to the use of colour. For example, if the logotype uses a combination of specified colours such as two Pantone-referenced ones, these have to be used on all publications and products, whether digital- or print-based. Colour can become an essential part of a brand identity – Cadbury's purple is on all its products and is trademarked to them to exclude its use by manufacturers of similar products.

These cans feature the same colours but, used differently, they help distinguish the standard drink from the diet variety.

Colour in Production

Even if a company bases its identity on one or two specific colours, the way the colours appear can vary according to whether they are used in a digital or print format, the type of stock they are printed on and the printing process. An example of this is a web site where the colour of a product varies according to the receiver's screen calibration and settings such as brightness and contrast. In print, a colour could look different depending on whether it is printed on cardboard or metallic foil. Different materials and printing processes are discussed in more detail in Chapter 7.

This range of Cadbury products, packaged using different materials, demonstrates the effect that the stock can have on the printed colour.

Case Study
Rock Guitar Styles,
John Clementson,
London and Brighton

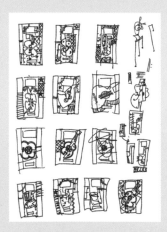

1.

To start with, John produced layout ideas in the form of small-scale thumbnails. In order to explore a range of design elements based on a guitar's shape and features, he experimented in black-and-white line, without including ideas for colour. Although he had colours in mind, based on the brightly coloured electric guitars used in rock music, he preferred to get his ideas down quickly and not make a final choice at this stage.

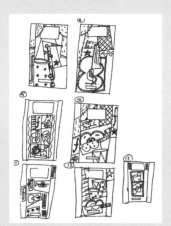

2.

John selected the more promising thumbnails for further refinement at a slightly larger scale, but continued to work in black-and-white line. Although he was becoming more certain about the colours he wanted to use, this is not explicit in the thumbnails as they were working drawings for his own use.

3.

Alongside this ideas development, John experimented with combinations of colours, such as analogous, primary and complementary, in order to decide on the palette that would fit best with the content of the albums.

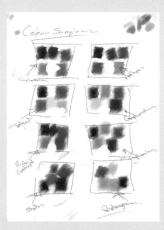

4.

John worked selected designs up to full size and started to indicate potential colour combinations, based on his previous experiments with colour. At this stage they are only annotations to the sketches as he was working quickly on several ideas.

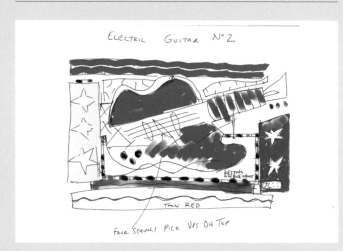

5.

Once John had sketched colour possibilities into the full-size line drawings it became clear that he was definitely using a palette of predominantly primary colours; both he and the client saw this as being appropriate to the theme of basic rock guitar styles. The infill of colour is still sketchy as the designer was working up several sketches at the same time.

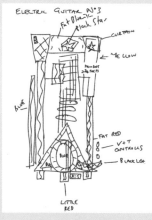

6.

This more detailed full-size rough gave a good indication of what the finished piece would look like. At this stage, the design was sufficiently resolved to enable the client to understand what the cover would look like when it was printed, which allowed John to produce the final artwork and move on to the production phase of the design process.

John Clementson was commissioned to design the covers for a series of three albums: *Rock Guitar Styles*. The brief required a 'chunky' style, using strong, simple images, that would work effectively at the small scale of a CD cover. As it was a series, rather than a one-off design, it was important that the colour scheme and style was fairly consistent across the whole series to provide cohesion and a sense of belonging to a set. This case study was chosen because it demonstrates an individual approach to the use of colour in that John chose to use flat areas of colour to enhance the compositions. He calls this particular method of working, his 'fuzzy felt' approach where he cuts out coloured shapes based on parts of the guitar

and then experiments with arrangements. This approach incorporates colour associations and different colour relationships such as complementary opposites.

7.

To produce the final artwork, John made a variety of alternative shapes by painting the different colours from his chosen palette on to pieces of foamboard. The board was rigid and light, which allowed for ease of cutting and also enabled the designer to experiment with combinations of various elements and colours. The thickness of the board gave the final images a semi-three-dimensional quality, which is characteristic of John's illustrations.

8.

Two of John's finished designs; combinations of elements are used, some of them common to both pieces and some individual. The strong, basic colours help to convey the rough, loud characteristics of rock music. The text is minimal and simple, leaving the strong, coloured shapes to dominate the designs.

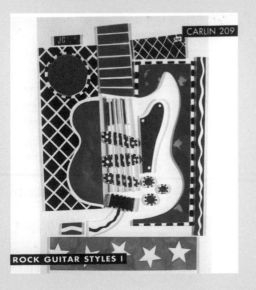

protégez l'enfant !

Automobile—Club de Suisse

Image Potential

6

Maximizing image potential is an important aspect of design, and this chapter describes how to do this, including selecting parts of images, and manipulating and editing images. It also discusses how images can be improved, which nowadays is usually done with software.

There are a number of ways in which images can be changed, ranging from retouching damaged or difficult areas, through adjusting contrast and colour, to deleting unwanted sections. Another approach is to change the appearance of the image overall by changing it from colour to black and white or from a tonal image to line.

But before you undertake any changes to an image, you need to ensure that it is of a high enough quality (resolution) which, in digital terms, is the dpi (dots per inch, normally used for print purposes) or ppi (pixels per inch, normally used for screen design) which was mentioned in Chapter 1. If you start with a low-resolution image, it is very difficult to improve it whereas a high-resolution image can be scaled down as required.

Opposite: a powerful design by Josef
Müller-Brockmann which uses contradiction
in scale and simple type to dramatic effect.

Scaling Images

There can be many reasons for scaling – decreasing or increasing an image's size. You may want it to be larger or smaller to fit in with the rest of your design. Alternatively, you may want to change its scale to create drama, or you may wish to change its size so that it relates to other images within a design.

Most scaling of images is now done digitally, and is one of the simplest processes to undertake. When doing this, however, it is worth remembering that any scaling will have an effect on the digital size of the image and it may be necessary to check that it will look the way you intend when it is printed. Also, what you see on the screen is not always what the image looks like when it is printed. Inkjet and laser printers vary considerably and printing can be affected by temperature, humidity, paper stock, calibration, colour mode and so on, so it is worth checking a printer's proof before committing to the change.

 When scaling an image, it is easy to distort it inadvertently and end up with something that differs from the original. You sometimes see images in newspapers or magazines that have been distorted so that people appear shorter and fatter or taller and slimmer than they are in reality. It is also bad practice to distort an image without permission, as discussed in Chapter 1.

It is important to know that changing the scale of an image can fundamentally change how it looks, depending on the sort of image used. A dense one that works well at a larger size may end up looking too dense at a smaller scale. This is because, as the image reduces in size the content condenses into a smaller space and therefore looks denser; this is referred to as filling in. It is particularly important to consider this if the image is to be printed on absorbent stock such as newsprint, where the ink literally fills in spaces and the image may look denser still. Conversely, when a large image made up of thin lines is reduced in size you may lose some of the lines.

When designing, it is a good idea to use low-resolution versions of your images as placeholders for the high-resolution versions needed at the finished printing stage. The lower-resolution images, with their smaller file sizes, may be placed and moved easily and quickly. The small file size also means that they are easier to print off in rough layouts during the design process.

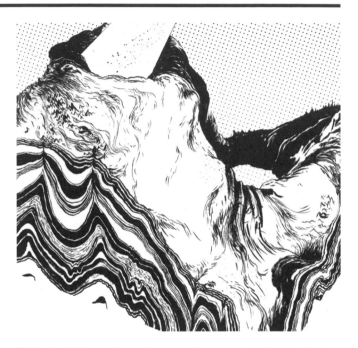

The fine detail may be lost from this illustration by Grandpeople when it is reduced in size. This problem would be exacerbated if an absorbent stock were chosen for printing.

Working size-up

When generating an image, it is often easier to work at a larger size than needed and then scale down the image when you are finished. This is referred to as 'working size-up' when the size is being doubled, but it's possible to work to any larger scale, depending on the image and personal preference. If you want to include detail in an image, working at a larger scale can make this easier and, conversely, if you want an image to appear looser and less detailed, working at a smaller scale and then scaling up helps to achieve this effect. There are some projects that necessitate working size-up, one of which is postage stamp design where it would be extremely difficult to work to the finished size, even of larger stamps.

 When working digitally, there is a temptation to work on sections of an image at a very large size when adding or adjusting detail. This is akin to working on part of a mural without seeing the whole, and means you are working in isolation and the section you are working on may end up at odds with the rest of the image. Don't forget to keep looking at the image in its entirety.

Activity

Select three images, one line, one tone and one full colour, as shown below. Experiment with different sizes for each image, either by photocopying it or using image manipulation software, increasing and decreasing the sizes so that you can compare them. You will need to print out your digital images as you will not be able to compare them easily on screen.

Cropping Images

A simple but effective way of making otherwise nondescript images more dynamic is by cropping them. This is where one portion of an image is emphasized by obscuring or deleting another portion. It is also used when parts of an image are superfluous or compete with the message that is being communicated. Cropping is often used in editorial matter to get more mileage out of an image by isolating a portion of it. In magazine design, for example, it is common practice to use an illustration for the introduction to an article, which is then visually linked through interesting crops of this illustration on subsequent pages throughout the magazine.

 Bear in mind that if you use an image more than once, even a detail, you may have to pay additional fees if it was sourced from a stock library.

Traditionally, L-brackets were used to help identify where to crop an image for the best effect, and symbols for L-brackets are used in many digital software cropping tools. However, not all cropping needs to conform to the confines of L-brackets; it can be much more intuitive and even random. If you think there is too much background to the right of a person, for example, you can just crop that part of the picture. Close cropping of images is often used to make them more dramatic or intimate, but this can result in them becoming decontextualized and even claustrophobic.

The designer is using L-brackets to decide which area of an image should be cropped.

A section of an image being cropped from the background using computer software.

Sometimes it is possible to decide which images need cropping at the outset of the design process, whereas at other times this will become apparent as the need arises or as the design suggests. Subject matter often influences the way an image is cropped in order to communicate the message. Cropping isn't always rectangular and hard-edged; an image is sometimes cropped into a circle or irregular shape, or it can have a soft edge, called a vignette. (A vignette is an image whose borders subtly fade away into a surrounding background.) ❶

It is also worth exploring different approaches, such as cropping a landscape photograph into a portrait format. This is like looking at an image afresh and can often open up creative possibilities for its use. Sometimes, an image can be cropped very tightly so that it changes from being recognizable into an abstract shape or pattern; this can be useful in the context of repeated or background images or to make a specific part of a design catch the viewer's eye.

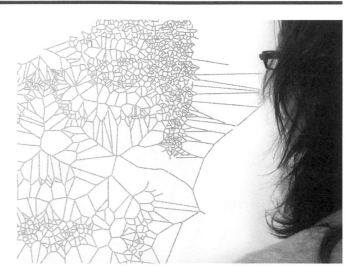

Richie Kuncyusk has cropped the person looking at the lettering image in order to direct attention to the main subject of the picture.

❶ Sahra Mesgna has made a vignette around the image within a dark background, to draw the viewer in.

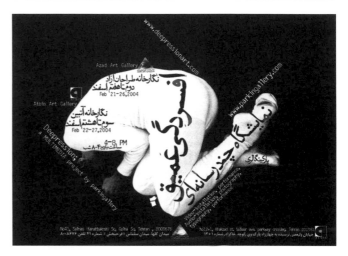

This image by Amirali Ghasemi for a poster advertising an exhibition has been cut from its background to maximize its impact.

This design by Annika Bitter uses a roughly cropped image superimposed on a gradient background to give a sharp angular outline leading into the information at the top of the page.

Cut-outs

Sections of images can be isolated, and used separately or for emphasis. If only one part of an image is needed, such as an eye or mouth, it can be cut out and incorporated into a design. This is often the case in magazines, where part of an image is used within the text; runarounds and cut-outs are discussed in Chapter 3.

A detail of the main image has been used on this double-page spread to draw the reader in and link the two pages. It is particularly effective as the painting's subject appears to be looking out at the reader.

Manipulating Images

Manipulating an image opens up creative potential in that an unusual approach or a different viewpoint can change a composition dramatically. The manipulation can be as simple as altering its colour or size or as complicated as combining several images into one. As well as size and scaling, described earlier in this chapter, and manipulation issues related to colour, discussed in Chapter 5, there are many other ways in which an image may be manipulated, such as by using the filter effects available in digital darkroom software. These include skewing, posterizing and morphing. The list is endless and is open to individual experimentation, so only a few specific examples are discussed here.

 It is easy to be seduced by new tricks in software but such tricks are used by everyone and quickly become gimmicky.

Many manipulation techniques have become commonplace and are simple to achieve using software that enables automatic changes at the click of a mouse. A good example is applying perspective to a group of objects. This used to entail redrawing the group but is now easily achievable by selecting the items and choosing from the options available, such as where to put the vanishing point.

Other effects include digital versions of traditional photographic retouching techniques such as dodging and burning, which increase or decrease the tone in an area of the image. On the other hand, some techniques, such as liquefying, texturizing and distorting, have evolved via software developments.

Many techniques are available within digital cameras, which provide all sorts of ways of cropping and changing an image before it leaves the camera. One of the most obvious is changing a colour image to black and white or introducing sepia tones to make an image look antique. In addition, software can be used to make a photograph look as if it has been produced in another medium, such as oil paint or ink, as well as in different artistic genres such as Impressionism or Pop Art.

In this example, John Marshall has used software filters to manipulate the original image in order to achieve a style that looks more appropriate to the subject rather than the studio lit effect of the original.

This photograph was taken in poor lighting but, as the brief was to capture the atmosphere of live performance, Parc&Maul manipulated the images using software. This involved cropping the image, altering brightness and contrast, removing overall red tint, increasing tonal variation, emphasizing detail as well as increasing the focus on the subject while making the background more abstract.

Software developments in photographic manipulation also enable existing images to be altered so that the message is communicated more effectively. This may be the case in instances such as using blurring to imply motion, or skewing or distorting an image, or parts of it, to make it more shocking.

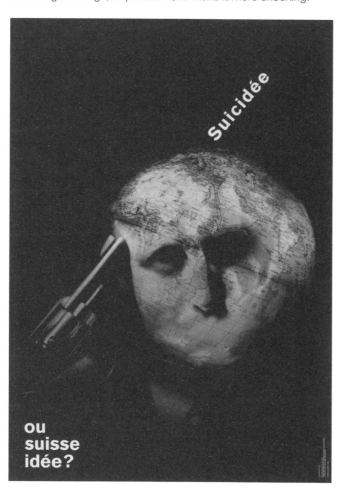

"Some kind of LA hard boiled; something" collage

Ed Fella uses found images to create his collages, as in this example.

Jean-Benoît Lévy has manipulated the original images and used shock to convey his message.

 As with any digital effect, these techniques are to be used with caution; like any emphasizing or attention-drawing device they can be overused.

Montage and collage techniques can be achieved both digitally and manually, and it is worth considering traditional methods as these can be very effective in achieving a tactile and hand-finished feel which may enhance some communications. Often, traditional and digital techniques are combined. Digital montage and collage effects can achieve exceptionally sophisticated results, and are also used in editing images.

Activity

Choose a fairly simple image; perhaps tear one from a magazine or use one of your own photographs. Tear a section out of the image, either from top to bottom or left to right.

Replace the missing section using any materials or techniques that you think appropriate.

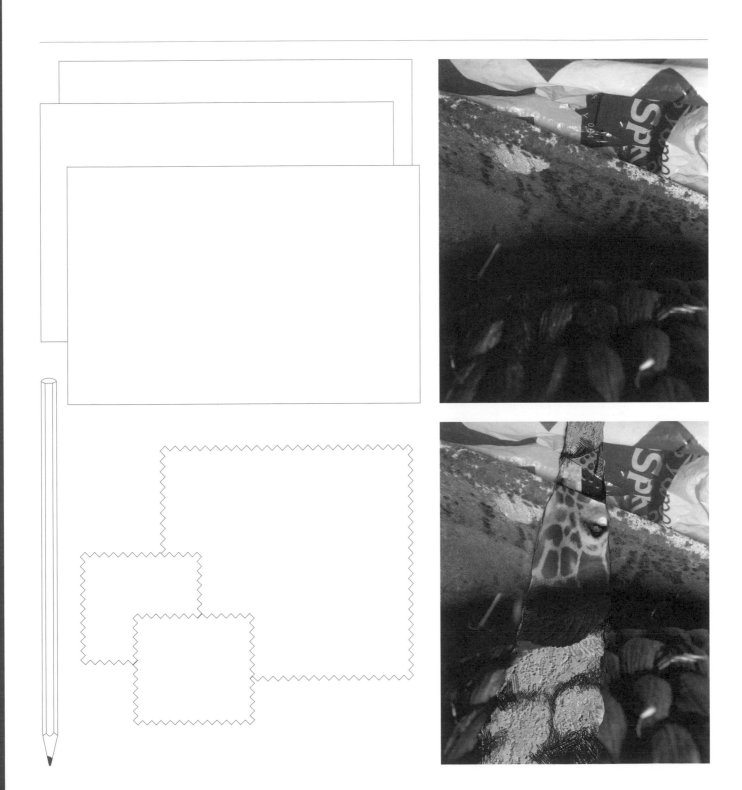

❶ Attak's cut-out in the image, shown opposite, shows how fine detail can be retained and isolated from any background interference.

Editing Images

Camera Angle and Viewpoint

In this image a low camera angle creates a feeling of power, with the figure looming over the viewer, making them feel small and intimidated.

This image also uses a low camera angle and distortion, but in this case it is used to amuse and entice the viewer.

Sahra Mesgna uses camera angle to reinforce the message of looking up.

These two images show the use of retouching: the rather sad looking pigeon of the original has been replaced with a much perkier specimen which adds to the lively feel of the picture.

Many of us have wanted to edit people out of our photograph albums at some time or other. With modern tools such as Photoshop it is possible to, literally, 'rub someone out'.

Editing applies to any change made to the original image, and could be as simple as adding a line or as complicated as cutting out around a fluffy kitten to remove the background. ❶

Retouching

Most photographs are subject to some form of editing before they go to print, even if this is just removing a speck of dust. Images for fashion magazines, for instance, are notoriously retouched in order to create the blemish-free look that we all aspire to and that sells the merchandise.

Editing and retouching are also useful in changing a message or the importance of an image's contents.

The angle from which a photograph is taken can make a difference to the way in which a subject is interpreted. At its most simple, a low viewpoint makes people seem more important and a high camera angle makes them seem less so. An example is photographs of executives in company reports, which may be taken from a low angle to make them look as if they are looking down, and conveys the message that they are powerful. These effects can often be achieved by using software to distort the image and make it look as if the photograph has been taken from another angle. Such effects can also be used for shock tactics.

Case study
Flowers in the Mirrors,
Hong Kong Science Museum,
Nicola Chang, Hong Kong

1.

These examples from Chang's workbook
show how the background image was
developed. The designer considered the
first image to be unsuccessful as an
unexpected black area was reflected in
mirrors. In the second example, the black
was replaced with yellow, which she
considered a better solution. In the final
example, the lighting was adjusted to
make the background image brighter.

2.

Another page from Chang's workbook
shows the background image and
the one-shot composite used in the
final design. These images show the
photograph that was used and the
cropped version, together with two
possible backgrounds.

Nicola Chang's commission was to produce designs for a special exhibition, 'Flowers in the Mirrors', at the Hong Kong Science Museum. The theme of the exhibition was reflection and symmetry, relating the concepts to the theme explored in a Chinese story 'The Fairy of the Hundred Flowers'.

The brief required an image that would work for a poster, outdoor banners, bunting, advertisements, opening backdrop, promotional backdrop, admission tickets, promotional folder, school-visit worksheets, web site and signage, all of which would incorporate image and text. The museum curators did not want the image to appear too digitally generated, so it was produced from one photographic shot and cropped to fit on to a separate background.

The designer used a symmetrical layout for the image, to reinforce the exhibition's title, and the imagery incorporates cropped images of flowers and dancing children to form an eye-catching and dynamic composite picture.

3.

The two images were combined using Photoshop. The cropped image was carefully examined and any imperfections were removed. The cut-out was placed on the yellow background image (top middle), but this was considered to be too plain and the background image was therefore manipulated to include flowers (as in the bottom two screenshots). The last screenshot, far right, shows the logo, with space at the bottom for text.

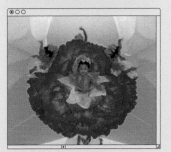

4.

This shows how the image was used on a poster, which was reproduced at various sizes, for example as a billboard on the side of a building.

5.

Here the image was used as an outdoor promotional banner. Chang used a limited amount of text, in order to keep the message simple and eye-catching.

Unrest
Jonathan Ellery

10th March —
22nd April 2007

Unrest, the latest body of work
from Jonathan Ellery. An exhibition
of ephemera, brass, sound and
moving image.

Opening hours
Daily: Noon – 10.30pm
Sunday: Noon – 5.30pm

www.thewappingproject.com

WAPPING

Production

7

Production is the final part of the design process but many reproduction and printing issues need to be resolved at the outset as they can dictate how images are used. If a design is destined for print production, for example, the stock and finishes to be used need to be considered early on. This chapter looks at these and other factors, such as the potential effects of different printing processes, binding, proofing and the various problems that can occur when colour is used in the production process. Some of these factors also affect designs destined for the screen.

❶ Martin Woodtli has provided contrast in this design, shown opposite, by increasing the size of a small printed image to such an extent that it has become blurred and indistinct, contrasting with the sharp edges of the rest of the elements of the design.

Image Size and Resolution

Whether for print or screen, it is essential to check the suitability of the original images to ensure that they will reproduce in the way you want them to. Often, when finishing artwork for production, what looks good on screen will not necessarily translate to high-resolution printing.

Size

The actual size of an image needs to be appropriate to the finished format. A good example of this is designing for something small, such as a postage stamp, when the maximum size you can work to is approximately A6, as anything larger would lose definition when scaled down. Conversely, it is difficult to scale a small design up to fit a larger format as the image may become distressed and quality will be reduced. This can, however, sometimes be used to good effect. ❶

This small stamp incorporates an image with a lot of detail. If the original image had been produced on a large scale, the detail would have been lost when it was reduced to fit the stamp's format.

FROMDOO RTODOOR

VEB-VOLKSEIGENER-BETRIEB-STADTGALERIE BERN

TAGDER ARBEIT

rundgang durch berner künstlerInnenateliers
am 1. mai und 2. mai 1999

Resolution

The difference between print and screen may influence the choice of images as their quality needs to be much higher for use in most print media than it does for screen. Checking the resolution of images is an important part of preparing a design for print.

Generally, the higher the resolution, the higher the quality. Resolution is usually expressed in terms of dots per inch (dpi) or, occasionally, lines per inch (lpi) and, in the case of digital images, pixels per inch (ppi). It refers to the amount of information the image contains so the more dots, pixels or lines per inch, the more detail.

Dpi is usually referred to in relation to printed matter and most printers require an image of 300 dpi or more to ensure good reproduction in high-quality print, as was the case with the images for this book. However, newspapers and magazines often require a much lower-resolution image, usually around 150 dpi. Lpi is another term used in printing, for tonal images, and relates to the number of printed halftone lines per inch that are printed; for example, around 85 lpi for newsprint (low quality) and 150–200 lpi for high-quality print. However, lpi is not often used nowadays as designers and printers tend to use either ppi or dpi.

Pixels per inch is the measurement used for digital image resolution and is often much lower than that needed for print because computer screens reproduce visual material in a different way. Whatever the resolution of a computer monitor, an image can only be reproduced to a certain standard and a low-resolution image therefore appears just as clear as a high-resolution one. When an image taken from a web site is printed it usually only reproduces well at a small size because of its low resolution. Another factor is that high-resolution images demand more processing power, and web site images are normally restricted to 72 ppi at 100 percent to ensure they load easily on most computers.

The difference between these two versions of the same image is that the first is reproduced at 300 dpi, which ensures that it is clear, whereas the second is at 72 dpi, resulting in loss of quality and clarity.

Stock Weight and Finish

The most obvious example of production determining how an image is used is where the stock chosen will not take it effectively. For instance, a very absorbent paper will not take detailed imagery because the ink will spread in a similar way to water on tissue paper; in this case, a simple image using blocks of colour or clear lines might be more effective.

There is a wide range of stock and substrates and many of them can add value to a design. A soft paper, for example, will not only handle differently to one with a hard gloss coating, it will also make an image appear less hard-edged or sharp. Textured or patterned-finish stock is often used to convey a hand-finished quality that complements natural or environmentally friendly products.

Images may be affected by the texture or surface quality of the stock, particularly if it has a strong raised pattern, loose strands such as fibres or any texture that has areas of deep indentation. In such instances the printing plate doesn't make good contact with the paper and areas of print may be missed. If you are using a textured paper you may consider selecting an image that does not have fine detail as this may be lost.

This winner of a Robert Horne Shout Award, by the Institute of Contemporary Arts, has printed slightly raised, dense ink onto a textured paper to give a tactile quality to the design.

This close up shows the effect of texture on print.

Before you file me under later, turn one page, Stephen awaits...

Opposite: this design uses Robert Horne
'Stephen' stock, which is aimed at the
environmentally conscious market as it has
a hand-produced, textured appearance.
This sort of stock works well with an image
that is produced to appear low resolution.

Weight

The thickness of the stock affects the feel of the printed piece, which can be important in tactile publications such as books or magazines. A thicker or heavier stock may impart a feeling of luxury or importance, but this can also apply to fine papers which, by their nature, are easily torn and therefore convey fragility and expensiveness. An example is a lightweight semi-transparent interleaf between pages in a book.

In some cases, very thick stock can make a publication more substantial and hard-wearing – examples are children's board books. Thicker stock is less prone to show-through, where the print on the other side of the paper can be seen. The weight of paper is usually represented in grams per square metre (gsm). When there is no show-through, images will not have any interference from matter printed on the reverse of the paper and will therefore appear clearer with good colour quality. Heavier papers lend themselves to images that need accurate reproduction of detail and colour.

 Most paper companies will supply samples and colour and weight swatches from their product range. They also provide information on the qualities of their paper with reference to print and handling. This can be very useful at the outset of designing as it can trigger ideas for texture and surface quality. It is worth keeping files of these samples for future reference, but bear in mind that new products will become available and some may go out of production, often depending on prevailing trends.

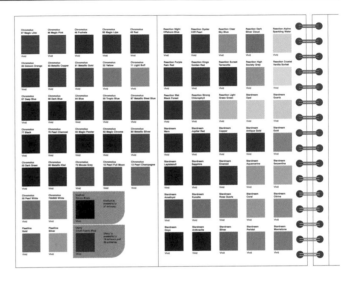

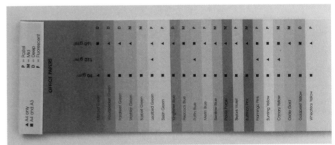

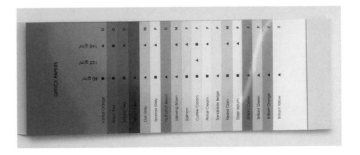

These are two examples of stock samples from Robert Horne. The top one is a series of chips showing the range of stock available and the bottom two are swatches showing the range of colours and weights available for a particular stock.

Stock finishes

As well as stock weight, it is useful to take other properties into consideration, such as finish. The finish on a stock can affect the choice of image used. For example, a coated paper will reproduce detail and fine line better than an uncoated one, which has a more absorbent surface. An image made up of areas of flat colour may benefit from an uncoated stock that does not show up reflections of lights or items in the vicinity, which may interfere with the flat colour. However, because uncoated papers are more absorbent than coated ones they are more likely to allow ink to spread or bleed beyond an image's boundaries.

Coated or uncoated does not necessarily mean the surface of the paper is shiny or matt, as many matt papers are coated. Stock is often referred to as matt, gloss or lustre, and can also be described as having a satin or silk finish. Other terms, such as laid or parchment, refer to the texture of the surface and often have their origins in the original materials and manufacturing process, which are now generally simulated. Other stock types such as onion skin, which is similar to tracing paper, or corrugated are used for specific purposes but have characteristics that offer creative potential.

Gloss and coated papers may be seen as being less environmentally friendly than uncoated stock because they go through more processes. However, this is not always the case and if you are concerned about these issues it is worth checking a stock's environmental credentials where possible, usually with the supplier or through the printer. Uncoated matt papers achieve an environmentally friendly look and tactile quality better than shiny, coated ones.

The reason the term 'stock' is used rather than paper is because it includes a range of materials, not all of which are paper-based, such as metallics and plastics. Metallics and plastics are also used as finishes on stock; the one that is probably most familiar is lamination, when a plastic coating is heat-sealed on to either one or both sides of the stock after printing. The process is usually used when durability and strength are required for a publication, such as a guide leaflet, that will be handled frequently.

These are two examples of overlay stock from Robert Horne. The first is semi-transparent and lightweight, similar to a heavy tissue or onion skin whereas the second is almost transparent, plastic and quite heavy.

In this example, corrugated card has been printed with a semi-transparent ink, giving it a more transitory, light feel appropriate to the recycling message.

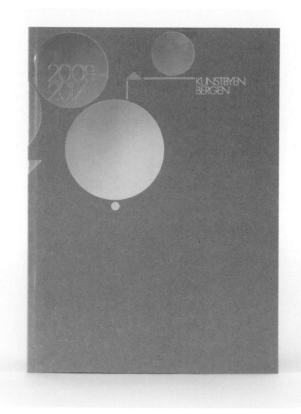

Grandpeople have used metallic ink, printed on uncoated, tactile stock, to highlight the shapes in this cover design.

Print finishes

There are a variety of print finishes such as UV (ultraviolet) varnish, embossing and thermography (a chemically raised ink surface) that can be used to enhance a design. UV varnish, for example, can apply sheen to an image so that it stands out from the design as a whole. These sorts of finish are often used for popular paperback covers as they add a tactile quality and help the design to stand out.

Other print finishes include debossing in which a design is stamped into a material and embossing where it is raised above the surface. Fluorescent inks can be used for emphasis in a similar way to metallics, and flocking can give a tactile quality to selected areas of a design. Die-cutting (cutting out areas of a design) is another post-production finish which, although expensive, can be very effective in concealing and revealing aspects of a design. Many examples of finishes can be seen in greetings cards where they may be combined or used in isolation.

Any choice of stock and print finishes needs to take into account the method of printing.

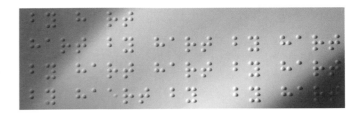

Embossing is used to produce Braille printing.

The figure zero has been die-cut out of the left-hand page to reveal the metallic finish print from the previous page.

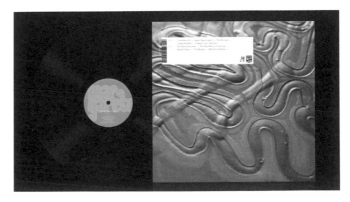

This vinyl cover design by Karl Martin Saetren uses a complex combination of embossing and metallic inks which would necessitate careful choice of stock prior to finalizing the design.

Print
Processes

Offset lithography, or litho, is currently the most commonly used commercial printing process. Without getting too technical, it is based on traditional lithography in which the design is transferred to a plate. This is attached to rollers which take up the printing ink and deposit it on the stock. The offset lithography process is designed for mass print production, whereas other print processes, although also designed to deliver multiples, are more craft-oriented and more suitable for limited print runs; there are often subtle differences between each print that give a hand-produced feel and convey exclusivity.

Such processes include woodcut, linocut, screen print, etching and drypoint, as well as letterpress which, although predominantly type-based, also includes images. One of the key features of these processes is the opportunities they provide to experiment and take risks, which is not practicable with commercial printing. They also have inherent qualities, such as block colour in screen print, and indentation or surface textures that can affect the feel and appearance of a hand-crafted print. Of course, it is also possible to incorporate these processes into designs that are subsequently printed in offset lithography in order to capitalize on such values. ❶ ❷

There are also the print processes that are in everyday use, both for business and in domestic situations: inkjet and laser printing. These are the ones that are most often used for proofing designs or for printing one-offs or small runs. Commercial printing, however, is changing rapidly and is adopting these technologies as they become cheaper, in the same way that developments in colour-printing technology over the past ten or so years has led to an increased use of full-colour printing.

❶ This linocut by Michael Neal uses layers of colour to produce an intricate image while retaining the tactile qualities of the medium.

This banknote illustrates the fine detail that may be achieved using an engraving technique for printing.

❷ This design by Adam Rix replicates the effect obtained in screen-printing when a mixture of ink colours is dragged across the screen. The work has an almost tactile quality.

INNOCENT SMOOTHIES

32.33

Whilst Mum is busy eating for two, for some reason Dad takes it upon himself to drink for two. We definitely wouldn't recommend this. Going out all evening, falling asleep on the train home, missing your stop, getting an expensive cab back, and trying to quietly sneak into bed won't win you any brownie points. Plus you should really be spending more time together – it won't be long before you're gagging for a quiet night in.

But boys will be boys, and so the brilliant people at innocent recommended this hangover-busting smoothie for any Dad who finds himself in such a position. If you can bear the rather unfriendly sound of a blender ringing in your ears, it might just save your liver, if not your relationship.

Activity

Experiment with readily available materials that will give a range of textures and effects. In the example shown below the student has experimented with potato prints, string prints and monoprints. She then scanned the chosen prints in order to compose a finished design on the computer. (A monoprint is usually produced by inking a sheet of glass and then drawing a design into the ink. A sheet of paper is placed over the glass and gently rubbed so that the design is transferred, in reverse, on to the paper.)

For this monoprint the student used a cut-up phone card to scratch designs into the surface of the ink.

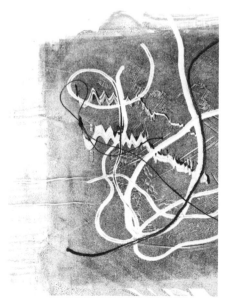

This print was obtained by placing a sheet of paper over the inked surface and applying pressure, either by using a roller or by another means.

This monoprint used a combination of plain and inked-up string on the surface in order to create different sorts of marks.

In this print the inked-up string was pulled from between the inked plate of glass and the paper while applying pressure to create this effect.

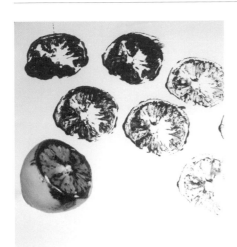

Prints may be obtained from a range of objects; in this case a lemon was cut and inked to provide the shapes but many different shapes and effects can be obtained using objects, for example leaves, mushrooms or textured cloth.

These prints were created using a potato cut in half with designs incised into the flat surface. This was then inked and stamped onto the paper. You could use other materials such as rubber or polystyrene as an alternative – these

would be more suitable for continual use as organic materials tend to deteriorate, sometimes very quickly.

The student scanned the various prints and combined them digitally to create a richly textured design. The original prints were produced in black and white as the student wanted to manipulate colour in the final stages of the design rather than having them predetermined by the original prints.

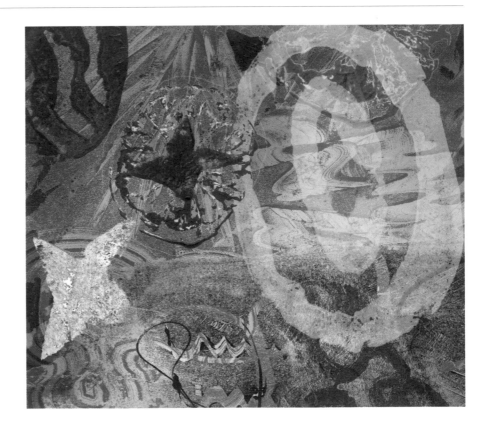

Colour in Production

A number of issues need to be considered when a design is being finalized. The major one is the difference between the appearance of the image on screen and once it has gone through the printing process – it is disappointing when a finished piece of work is returned from printing and the contrast is much darker or lighter than it looked on screen. Calibrating your monitor with your print output will help to alleviate this kind of problem, but is not normally possible when a commercial printing house is involved. Such printers usually provide a printer's proof for you to check colour among other things.

It is worth mentioning that many images are in RGB format, which is fine for reproduction on screen, but the colour may vary when they are converted to CMYK for commercial printing. For a specified set of colours (such as when matching to a company logo colour), one of the colour referencing systems, such as Pantone®, can be used. These assign a reference number to the colour mix and provide sets of reference swatches, just like a paint company. Most design software provides a digital version of these swatches, which may be used together with work in CMYK mode, as part of their toolbox.

If an image is produced digitally or scanned for print it should normally be converted to CMYK in order to conform with the printing process, which converts an image into the four process colours: cyan (C), magenta (M), yellow (Y) and black (K). This applies to conventional printing methods and not to the more recent digital print processes which use inkjet or recent and emerging print technologies for reproduction. Such technologies do not break colours down into CMYK screens, but blend them through the technical process.

When designing for screen there is little or no control over how colour appears on the recipient's screen as their monitor may be calibrated entirely differently. It is worth bearing this in mind when selecting colours and, if a design is intended for a wide audience, as with web site design, not being too specific about colour or tone. Colours are usually in RGB format as this is the way they will be reproduced, and most digital cameras produce images in this format.

 Most design software provides the option of setting colours as RGB or CMYK. It is worth checking these settings when you start working on a design and adjusting them for the production method you are designing for.

This star is misregistered with the background, leaving a white edge exposed.

Registration

One problem that may arise with colour printing is registration, where the printing plates have to align correctly to ensure a clear and accurate reproduction. An example of poor registration is when a plate is misaligned in newspaper or magazine printing: this causes one of the colours to be printed out of line with all the others, making the final print difficult to read and sometimes look visually disturbing.

The deliberate misaligning of a print layer or colour in an overprint can sometimes be used to good effect, as it can add layers, depth and texture, and is often combined with semi-transparent inks. Such effects can be simulated using software programs but, as with all effects, they need to be used with caution as overuse reduces impact.

Related to registration is ink trapping, where two colours meet. Trapping ensures that there is a gap in the first colour to be printed that is filled by the overprinted colour without any change to either colour. This is usually done automatically in desktop publishing programs provided you ensure that it is enabled in the preferences. Enabling usually means finding the document preferences and ensuring that the option for trapping is on. If trapping is not enabled, there is a possibility that a white gap will appear where two colours butt up to each other. If in doubt regarding trapping or other registration issues, it is wise to consult the printer for advice.

Related to trapping, and often treated as the same, is knock-out, where the first, or underlying colour, is completely removed where the two colours overlap.

www.jazzwerkplaats.nl

STICHTING JAZZ

sinds 1992

WERKPLAATS DEN BOSCH

DE STICHTING JAZZWERKPLAATS DEN BOSCH
zet zich, sinds de oprichting in 1992, actief in voor de
promotie van Jazz in 's-Hertogenbosch. Dit doen zij
door op eigen initiatief activiteiten te organiseren.
Daarnaast zoekt zij ook actief samenwerking met
partijen in het culturele veld om gezamenlijk ideeën
te ontwikkelen en initiatieven te nemen. Tenslotte
adviseert en ondersteunt zij andere culturele
instellingen bij initiatieven op het gebied van
geïmproviseerde muziek. Een aantal initiatieven
behoort ondertussen tot het standaard aanbod van
de Jazzwerkplaats.

Binding

For editorial matter, the final stage of the print process is usually binding. The methods used include stitching, where the pages are stapled or stitched together across the centre; perfect binding, where they are collected into sections and glued across the spine; and case binding, where pages are stitched in sections and the sections are stitched together across the spine. There are also many variations, such as stab binding.

The type of binding used depends on variables such as the number of pages, thickness of stock, size and format of the publication, and cost. There are also ergonomic considerations about the way a publication is to be handled and its intended use. Some large or thick books need the kind of binding used for hardbacks in order to give them stability, whereas a smaller book will remain usable with a soft cover. Hard or soft covers may indicate value, which is usually reflected in the price, and the same can apply to the use of traditional stitched bindings or perfect binding. Different types of binding affect the look of the page and how margins are used. A thick book, for example, may need a wider inner margin to prevent the spine breaking and ensure that content near the spine is visible. ❶

The type of binding can affect how an image is used. For example, if it is intended for use across an entire double-page spread, it will work better if it is on the centre-page spread of a stapled magazine, where it will be printed across both pages, than if it is in a book where it is split by the way the pages join the spine – which may result in the pages being misaligned and the halves of the image not matching. This is sometimes acceptable where the split is not obvious, but would not look good if the image included important information in the area of the split, such as a person's face. In addition, the reader may not be able to see the entire image without opening the book and flattening it, which risks damaging the binding. The same caveats apply when only part of an image continues across the spine. ❷ ❸

❶ Opening a double-page spread from a thick book with deep spine margins.

❷ On this double-page spread, the image has been printed across one sheet which is at the centre of a stapled publication and therefore may be seen in its entirety.

❸ In this double-page spread by Helen Shillabeer, the image has been printed on separate pages and is not fully visible at the centre where the pages join to the spine in a perfect binding.

Examples of standard bindings.

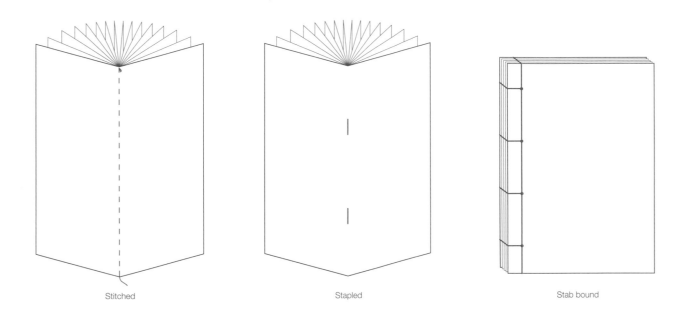

Stitched   Stapled   Stab bound

Perfect bound   Case bound

Before Production

When a design is finished, it is worth leaving it for a while and coming back to it with fresh eyes before checking details such as resolution. If your time is limited, looking at the design in a mirror (or reversing it on a computer), or squinting at it (snake eyes), will help you to see it from a different viewpoint and spot problems or things that need tweaking. These can relate to layout or design issues, such as one image not relating to another, or the wrong choice of colour used for emphasis. There may also be technical issues, such as an incorrect alignment of text and image or a margin that is too narrow or wide.

Pre-flight

The term pre-flight refers to preparation prior to sending to the commercial printer. The term derives from pre-flight checks on aeroplanes which are vital for safety. Although we are not suggesting that insufficient preparation prior to printing would have the same potentially disastrous results as a poor pre-flight check for an aeroplane, it can be pretty devastating and expensive if your finished artwork is inadequately prepared for printing.

When you are satisfied that the design is as you intended, check that the screen resolution/size (dpi or ppi) is correct, and that you have collected fonts, images and any other items needed for output. This applies to designs for both print and screen, and most design software packages have a facility that does this. It is important to organize these items and not move them around on the computer once they have been collected for output, so that the software program can locate them.

Proofing

A critical look at a proof printed on an inkjet or laser printer is a useful check before a design is finalized for production, and the proof can be used as a reference when the project is discussed with the printer or web designer. It should include clear instructions so that they have a good idea of what is expected of them. For example, if an image is cut out of a larger original, it is worth making a note to this effect on the proof. If you have used any special colours, such as PMS (Pantone® Matching System), ensure that the printer is aware of this, and mark areas of such colour on the printed proof. Information about the sort of stock specified and any particular finishes, such as UV varnish, should also be marked on the proof to provide additional guidelines for the printer.

Here Swiss-based master printer Tom Blaess is seen proof-checking a lithographic print coming off a flatbed offset press.

It is worthwhile keeping a copy of this proof to check against the finished product. Commercial printers normally produce printer's proofs to check colour and quality with the designer and client. It is good practice to obtain the client's signature on each of the proofs before committing them to print. Mistakes spotted post-production are costly, and sometimes impossible, to correct.

When checking printer's proofs (digital or photographic), bear in mind that stock quality, type and weight will affect the appearance of the print. Proofs are usually produced on a particular type of stock that doesn't take into account surface texture or absorbency of the stock the design will be printed on. Although what are known as 'wet proofs' are produced at the start of a print run, as a final check, finding mistakes at this stage can be expensive in terms of both time and cost as alterations mean changes to the plates and even further proofing.

When working with a web site developer, it is important to ensure they know what your intentions are for the final design; this information can take the form of screenshots and a flow chart. Screenshots are usually presented in the same way as proofs, and act as a check on the appearance of individual pages. A flow chart is essential for a web developer to work from as it is a visual guide to the structure of the design.

Digital Tips

Software is an important part of a designer's toolkit and the information that follows is useful in both print and screen design.

Resizing

Although it is not good practice to increase the size of digitally captured images such as photographs or scans because of the resulting loss of quality, when you are dealing with vector-based images, such as those produced with Adobe Illustrator, there may be more flexibility as these can be scaled up or down without loss of quality. Pixels do not offer this flexibility as they stay at the same size when an image's scale is changed.

Organizing files

When resizing an image or changing it in any way, always use the 'Save as' option and give the file a different name. It is usually easier just to assign a number after the name. However, if you have sourced the image from elsewhere, and it has a long name, it is worth shortening the filename of the original file before you start. This will help when you search for files because dialogue boxes often show only part of a filename unless they are expanded manually. Assigning a number to each change enables you find the latest version without having to expand the dialogue box or access the last date the file was modified.

It is important to be systematic and tidy when organizing files – the last thing anyone working to a pressurized deadline needs is having to search through masses of images scattered all over their computer. All files should be stored in a series of folders clearly labelled with the job you are working on. This is also good practice with physical files, such as transparencies and original artwork. It is important to ensure that you are systematic when you are collecting your files to output or performing a pre-flight check.

Backing up files

Whether a design is for print or screen, it is wise to make a back-up of the work. This cannot be stressed strongly enough or too many times: don't rely on movable storage media such as flash drives, and don't work off them; they are for back-up purposes. Always transfer files to the hard drive before working, then back them up to the storage device when you've finished.

An image file may be corrupted or damaged in storage, or while you are working, so a back-up copy is essential. It may mean you have to begin again if you were manipulating an image, but it saves having to source another copy of the image.

If you have an extended break while working on a design, such as a weekend away, it is worth making a back-up copy and taking it with you and/or storing it. If you work on a portable device such as a laptop, it is even more important to keep a separate back-up in case it is stolen, for instance, or you leave it on a train.

File formats: which ones and when?

The most common transferable file formats for images are JPEG, TIFF and EPS.

JPEG (joint photographic experts group) – This is probably the most common format as it is used by most digital cameras and is a compressed file. The advantage of JPEG images is that the file is generally small and therefore more portable and manageable, ideal for web use. This is important if you are sending files as attachments to emails.

TIFF (tagged image file format) – This file format is generally used by professional designers and image makers as it is a more flexible format for halftone and photographic images. However the files do tend to be larger and are unsuitable for sending via email unless you are using a file compressing facility.

EPS (encapsulated postscript) – This is an encapsulated format and usually is used for vector or object-based artwork. The advantage is that it is smaller in size but allows flexibility in sizing and distorting, particularly flat colour and line, such as Adobe Illustrator files. The most common disadvantage of this file format is that, because the image is encapsulated, you can't easily change the content.

PNG (portable network graphics) and **GIF** (graphical interchange file) format – These file formats use a reduced number of specific colours and are designed for screen use. The advantage of these formats is that they can be animated and can have a transparent background.

Other file formats that you may come across are software-specific files such as Adobe Photoshop PSD (photoshop data file), Coral Painter RIFF (resource interchange file format), etc. These file formats are active which means that they save the image and its history and current settings which is useful if you want to take a break from a project and return to where you left off. The disadvantage is that they can become extremely large and unwieldy, making the transportation and sharing of them more difficult.

Warnings

The warning about warnings is: don't ignore them. Quite often, a warning icon pops up when digital files are being saved. A warning can be about a problem such as a colour that won't be the same when you change the file format, or it can be as simple as a reminder to flatten the layers in a Photoshop file, thus limiting the size of the file. ❶

Warnings you won't get

You will not normally get a specific warning about the size of files, but it is important to check that the file size is appropriate for its intended use. Small file sizes and the problems they can cause have already been discussed, but large file sizes can also cause difficulties as they take longer to process and use up more memory. This is something to watch out for, particularly if you are working on a computer that has limited processing power or storage capacity.

❶ This warning indicates that the colour used is out of gamut, or colour range, for printing purposes.

Case Study

Bastardised,
Bunch Design, London,
Croatia, Singapore

Bunch Design created *Bastardised*, a book of images which in their words 'epitomises the contemporary practice of communication design…', as a rebranding exercise. This reflects the sort of work Bunch are involved with, which includes graphic design, branding and packaging design. Bunch initiated a project aimed at developing a community of designers. They devised a brief around the theme of 'Made in Bunch' and sent it to fellow designers and illustrators, asking each of them to produce an image or logo for Bunch, with the intention of posting all the contributions on their web site. The web site attracted a wider audience, which resulted in more people participating in the project. Bunch were happy with the

1.

For the cover design, Bunch asked the designer Omega!TheKidPhoenix to realize their idea of putting 'astardised' inside the letter B to form the title of the book – *Bastardised* – which had been chosen to reflect the brief, which had, in effect, been to bastardise their logo.

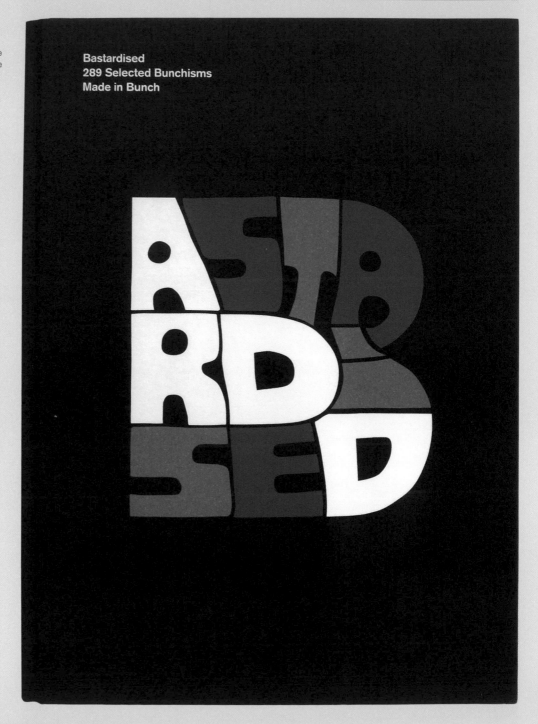

Bastardised
289 Selected Bunchisms
Made in Bunch

range of interpretations of their brief, which they considered to be bastardisations, or variations, of their identity.

The success of the project led Bunch Design to pull together the best, or their favourite, designs in a publication. To do this, they needed to get the agreement of all the designers/illustrators whose work would be included. This proved to be a long-winded, three-month process. Once all the participants had given their consent, Bunch were able to concentrate on the design of the book. They wanted the book to be simple in format, letting the works speak for themselves. They decided on a size of 170 × 235 mm (6 ½ × 9 ¾ in) as this seemed to work well with the thickness of the total number of pages (208)

which they had worked out by constructing a mock-up. This thickness was predetermined by the weight of the stock that was used. Bunch liaised with the printer and agreed on 170 gsm stock, which would give each page a substantial feel (standard photocopier paper is 90 gsm). As the images were the focus of the publication, Bunch Design used a plain typeface, Berthold Akzidenz Grotesk, for any text in the book. This was a logical choice as it is their corporate typeface.

2.

The designers took care to select and place complementary images or, in their words, 'bunchisms', together on the double-page spreads. They wanted to ensure that each image or logo had enough white space around it to allow it to stand alone and not be influenced by adjacent images.

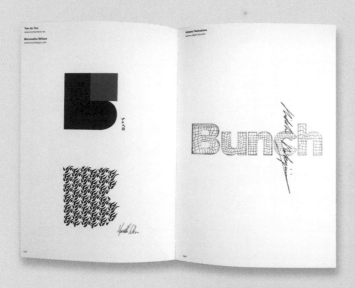

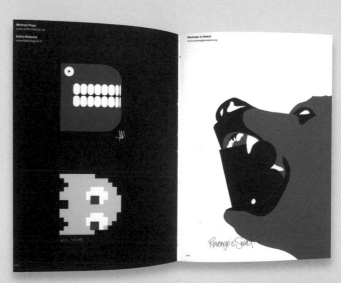

3.

The inside covers and fly papers (endpapers) were used to display images of Bunch Design merchandise, such as T-shirts and mugs, and images related to the production of *Bastardised*.

Once the pages had been designed, Bunch ran a pre-flight check to ensure all the images and text were ready for the printer. This included making sure images were at the correct resolution and size for the finished publication. It was also necessary to check that everything was in CMYK mode ready for four-colour printing.

After careful consideration, a matt stock – Maxi Offset 170 gsm paper – had been chosen for the pages of the book, as being the most suitable for the variety, colour and type of images to be included. *Bastardised* is a case-bound hardback and the 3 mm (⅛ in) thick cover boards were finished in Maxi Silk 120 gsm stock, then matt laminated.

4.

The printer provided proofs and a dummy book for proofing prior to production. This enabled the designers to find and correct errors that would have been missed on screen. It also allowed them to check that all aspects of the artwork, including colour and layout, were as intended.

5.

After this proofing stage the team from Bunch Design went to the printers to see the first run off the press. They felt this was the hardest part of the process, as they had to be quick to spot any problems – for example, by checking the optimum colour saturation for each of the CMYK colours – so that the printer could make adjustments.

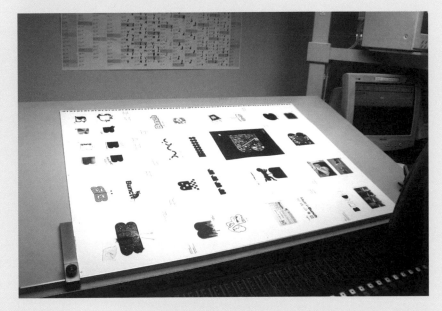

6.

Bastardised was printed in Croatia by Kratis, with paper sponsored by Igepa.

Glossary

A2, A4, A5 etc.
System of standardizing paper sizes that is commonly used in most countries apart from Canada and the United States. It begins with A0, which measures 841 x 1189 mm; for each subsequent size the longer measurement is halved so A1 measures 594 x 841 mm. This continues to A10 which measures 26 x 37 mm. The US system is more complicated with paper measured in inches and the standard letter size, equivalent to A4, is 8½ x 11 in (216 x 279 mm). They have many other sizes in common use including Legal (216 × 356 mm), Executive (190 × 254 mm), and Ledger/Tabloid (279 × 432 mm).

Bas-relief
Picture, often formed from clay, in which elements are carved or sculpted on a background which is less than half of its full depth, i.e. in low relief.

Baseline
The invisible line at the base of a line of text on which the letters sit.

Burning
Photographic technique for darkening an area of an image.

Case bound
A form of bookbinding where the pages are stitched in sections and these sections are then stitched together across the spine. These are then encased in a cover which attaches to the book itself via endpapers.

Centre-page spread
The centre pages of a stapled publication.

Clip art
Royalty free images that are often provided with software for use in documents and presentations.

CMYK
Acronym for the colours, cyan (C), magenta (M), yellow (Y), black (K), that make up the colours of the four-colour printing process.

Counterform
A counterform is the space left within letterform shapes such as the space in the centre of a Q or p.

Debossing
Where a design is stamped into the substrate, giving an indented effect.

Die-cutting
Where a section of a design is cut out, often to reveal the material underneath, using a special metal form called a die.

Distorting
Changing or exaggerating an image's shape, usually through a digital process.

Distressing
The technique of destroying or manipulating an image with the aim of making it look old or damaged.

Dodging
Photographic technique for lightening an area of an image.

Double-page spread
Two pages of a publication that are viewed adjacent to each other, as in page 2 and 3 of most magazines, for example.

dpi
The quality of an image; its resolution, in terms of the number of visible dots per inch. The closer together the dots, the more dots there are per inch which results in higher quality.

Drypoint
A technique used in printmaking where the design is scratched into the soft metal plate which forms the area that is printed.

Embossing
Where a design is stamped into the reverse of the substrate giving a raised or low-relief effect.

Endpaper
The pages of the book that lie next to the covers, usually in case-bound publications where they are integral to the inside cover paper. These may often be treated as a decorative element.

Etching
Printmaking technique where the image is etched into the plate, usually with acid, forming the area to be printed.

Fibonacci series
A series of numbers where each number is the sum of the preceding two; often occurs in nature.

Flat plan
A diagram of the pages of a publication laid flat which is used by designers to help them work out how to arrange the various elements of the publication and provide an overview of the entire work.

Flow chart
A diagram showing the structure of a web site or multimedia artefact.

Fly paper
See Endpaper.

Footer
Text appearing consistently at the base of each page of a publication or part of a publication, often with the page number.

Golden section
A proportional relationship of roughly 8:13 which is considered well balanced and pleasing on the eye.

Grid
The underpinning structure for the page layout of most text-based design, usually made up of columns of text.

gsm
The weight of paper as represented in grams per square metre (gsm), irrespective of size.

Halftone
A tonal image that is represented by lines made up of a pattern of dots of varying sizes.

Header
Text appearing consistently at the top of each page of a publication or part of a publication.

Ideogram
An image or symbol used to represent a concept or action, conveying an abstract notion, rather than a depiction of an object or person.

Illuminated manuscript
An early writing where the text was 'illuminated' with illustrations to enhance or explain the story, often embellished with precious substances such as gold.

Indexed colour
A way of managing the colour in digital images to save computer memory: the colour is stored indirectly in a file called a GIF. The downside of this system is that it only provides a limited number of colours to work with.

Information bar
A section of information, separate from the main text, which includes information relevant to the article. It is usually included in a separate box or highlighted area.

Ink trapping
Where two colours meet, the lighter colour overlaps the darker colour fractionally to ensure that no gaps appear between colours if there is any mis-registration during printing.

Lab colour
Lab colour (or lab mode) is used in computers to simulate the way humans see colour in order to obtain good colour balance. 'L' stands for luminance, 'a' represents how red or green a colour appears and 'b' represents how blue or yellow a colour appears.

Laminating
Covering or encasing an image with a clear film to seal it, often for strength or to prevent marking.

Leading
The space between lines of type (also called line spacing) from one baseline to the next.

Letter spacing
The space between letters.

Letterform
The shape of an individual letter of the alphabet.

Letterpress
A method of relief printing where the letterforms are raised in metal or wood type to form an area where the ink can be applied before printing.

Line spacing
The space between lines of type (also called leading) from one baseline to the next.

Linocut
A method of printmaking where the areas not to be printed are cut out from the surface of lino.

Liquefying
A technique developed in computer software that allows the user to draw over an image, distorting areas so that they appear as if they are dissolving or swirling in liquid.

Logotype
A design developed from a company's or institution's name or emblem which forms its visual and/or corporate identity.

lpi
The number of printed halftone lines per inch that are printed. The more lines per inch, the better the resolution of the image and therefore its quality.

Matt laminate
Covering or encasing an image with a clear matt-finished film to seal it.

Moodboard
A method of combining items such as images and objects to visually express the feel of a design, for example in terms of colour or texture.

Multichannel
This colour mode, used in photographic manipulation software, allows the user to include extra colour channels while working on an image, which is useful, for example, when working with complicated spot colour.

Negative space
The spaces left between or around shapes and forms.

Overprint
Printing a colour on top of another colour.

Pictogram
An image that represents an object or a person.

Positive space
The spaces created by a shape or form.

ppi
pixels per inch (ppi) is the measurement used for digital image resolution. Similar to dpi, the higher the ppi, the higher the resolution/quality.

Pull quote
A short section of text, a phrase or quote, pulled out of an article in order to draw attention to the content.

Resolution: high, medium, low
The quality of the reproduction of an image, either for screen or print. High resolution means that the image has higher definition and clarity for good-quality print-based work whereas, at the other end of the scale, low resolution means an image will be less defined and therefore only suitable for use in screen-based work. There are a range of resolutions in between which are suitable for different types of publication and print processes. See also dpi, lpi and ppi.

RGB
An acronym for red green blue, the three colours that make up the digital colour range.

Screen print
A method of printing where ink is pushed through a fine mesh (screen), to which a stencil has been attached, on to the stock to form the image.

Storyboard
A storyboard is used by designers and illustrators to provide a sense of the narrative. Storyboards are often used for animation sequences, short films and videos including advertisements.

Style sheet
Enables the designer to apply specific attributes, such as choice of typeface or leading, to different sections of a publication.

Template
A predetermined structure which provides the basic information, for example a grid, to which different content may be applied.

Texturizing
A technique available in photographic manipulation software that applies various textures to an image, implying a tactile quality.

Thermography
A printing process that uses heat-sensitive ink to create a raised surface (see also Embossing).

Trim marks
Marks used in the printing process to indicate where the printed paper is to be cut to finished size or folded.

Typestyle
The different style that may be applied to a typeface such as bold, where the letterforms are made denser, or italic, where the letterforms are sloped.

UV varnish
A clear varnish applied as a printed layer to the surface or selected areas of a design and then cured under ultraviolet light.

Vignette
An image that fades out into the background.

Wet proof
A proof produced using the plates and stock that will be used for the actual printing job.

White space
The area of a design that does not contain any elements (the space may not necessarily be white).

Woodcut
A method of printing where the image is produced by carving into the surface of a woodblock, leaving a raised area that is inked.

Further Reading

Josef Albers, *Interaction of Color*, Yale University Press, 2006

Association of Illustrators, *The Illustrator's Guide to Law and Business Practice*, Association of Illustrators, 2008

Jeremy Aynsley, *Pioneers of Modern Graphic Design*, Mitchell Beazley, 2001

Bo Bergström, *Essentials of Visual Communication*, Laurence King Publishing, 2008

Daniel Chandler, *Semiotics: the basics*, Routledge, 2007

Dr. Nigel Chapman and Jenny Chapman, *Web Design: A Complete Introduction*, John Wiley & Sons, 2006

Douglas Cockerell, *Bookbinding and the Care of Books: A Handbook for Amateurs, Bookbinders and Librarians*, Lulu.com, 2009

David Dabner, *Graphic Design School: The Principles and Practices of Graphic Design*, Thames & Hudson, 2004

Edith Anderson Feisner, *Colour*, Laurence King Publishing, 2006

Phil Baines and Andrew Haslam, *Type and Typography, Second Edition*, Laurence King Publishing, 2005

Andrew Haslam, *Book Design*, Laurence King Publishing, 2006

David Hornung, *Colour: A Workshop for Artists and Designers*, Laurence King Publishing, 2004

Scott Kelby, *The Adobe Photoshop CS4 Book for Digital Photographers (Voices That Matter)*, New Riders, 2008

Alan and Isabella Livingston, *The Thames & Hudson Dictionary of Graphic Design and Designers (World of Art)*, Thames & Hudson, 2003

Joyce Macario, *Graphic Design Essentials*, Laurence King Publishing, 2009

Philip B. Meggs and Alston W. Purvis, *Meggs' History of Graphic Design*, John Wiley & Sons, 2006

Quentin Newark, *What Is Graphic Design? (Essential Design Handbooks)*, Rotovision, 2007

Alan Pipes, *Foundations of Art and Design, Second Edition*, Laurence King Publishing, 2008

Alan Pipes, *Production for Graphic Designers, Fifth Edition*, Laurence King Publishing, 2009

Yolanda Zappaterra, *Editorial Design*, Laurence King Publishing, 2007

Web sites

www.lynda.com
(For software training)

www.colormatters.com/
colortheory.html

www.roberthorne.co.uk
(Information about stock)

www.theaoi.com
(The Association of Illustrators)

www.dandad.org

http://acid.eu.com
(Intellectual property protection)

www.dacs.org.uk
(Design and artists copyright society)

www.vads.ac.uk
(Online resource for visual arts)

www.good-tutorials.com
(Software tutorials)

Acknowledgements

Thanks to all those who contributed images, with special thanks to Bunch Design, Grandpeople, Jean-Benoît Lévy, Ludovic Balland, Nicola Chang, Parc&Maul, Sean Bird and Zane Manasco.

Thanks to our editors Helen, Anne and Sophie at Laurence King for guiding us through the process.

Thanks to our partners Mike and Carol for putting up with us (all the lunches Mike), to Carol Cooper, Emma Alsop and John Marshall.

Picture Credits

6: Anna Francescutti, illustration on desire based on a quote from *Atlas Shrugged* by Ayn Rand: 'One must make one's own desire and every shape of its fulfilment'. 8tl: 88160968 Â© 2009 Jupiterimages Corporation. 8tr: 36960810 Â© 2009 Jupiterimages Corporation 8bl: 88273393 Â© 2009 Jupiterimages Corporation. 9tl: Lindsey Marshall. 9tr: 88061468 Â© 2009 Jupiterimages Corporation. 9b: 000007016019 © iStockphoto.com/ Claudio Divizia. 10: 000005933577 © iStockphoto.com/Brandon Laufenberg. 11t: Creative Agency: Cogent Elliott / Art Director: Simon Fones / Client: Arriva Buses. 11m: Nicola Chang / Hong Kong Science Museum. 11b: Luke Coker. 12: Matthew Day (RSA Postage Stamp Winner 07/08). 13t: Amnesty International. 13b: Johan van der Acker Texiefabriek Germert, The Netherlands / www.vanderAcker.nl with thanks to Paul Battle of F.R.Street Ltd. www.streets.co.uk. 14-15: Dominique Milherou / www.petit-carnet.com. 16: UPM-Kymmene web site / www.upmforestlife.com. 17t: Creative director: Astrid Stavro / Art director: Astrid Stavro / Designers: Astrid Stavro, Rosanna Vitello, Cynthia Furrer. 17bl: 000002973982 © iStockphoto.com/Graham Dargie. 17br: Reproduced from 'Touchy-Feely ABC' by permission of Usborne Publishing, 83-85 Saffron Hill, London EC1N 8RT, UK. Copyright © 2010 Usborne Publishing Ltd. 18: Pictures courtesy www.davidpearsondesign.com / Great Loves No. 01: Doomed Love. No. 02: Forbidden Fruit. No. 04: Of Mistresses, Tigresses, and Other Conquests. No. 07: First Love. Cover illustrations by Victoria Sawdon / Great Loves No. 06: The Seducer's Diary. No. 18: Eros Unbound. Cover illustrations by David Pearson. 20l: Amnesty International. 20r: John Seth Marshall. 21: Martin Woodtli. 22: Martin Woodtli. 23: Design: Grandpeople / Illustration: Grandpeople / Client: Oslo Architects Association. 24: John Clementson / Client: Carlin Production Music/Destiny Music / Job: promotional poster / Art Director: Paul Kinane / Media: collage. 25t: Bunch Design / Agency: Content UK. 25b: Getty Images / SuperStock, Inc. 27t: 9256754 Â© 2009 Jupiterimages Corporation. 27b: 49782524 Â© 2009 Jupiterimages Corporation. 28: Lindsey Marshall. 29: Image courtesy of The Advertising Archives. 31: Inksurge, We Strive for Gold is the Tiger Beer's Gold, transatlantic book/ exhibition. 32–33: Ludovic Balland / © Ludovic Balland. All rights reserved. 34: Studio8 Design 36tl: Landmarks in Humanities by Gloria K. Fiero / Courtesy and © 2009 The McGraw-Hill Companies,Inc. All rights reserved / Designed and produced by Laurence King Publishing Ltd. 36tr and br: Joshua Gidman. 38: Jenny Tune. 39t and b: John Clementson / Client: Studio Editions (UK)/Harcourt Brace (USA) / Job: spread from a children's book written by Michael Rosen / Media: cut paper collage. 40l: Lindsey Marshall / Photography by John Seth Marshall. 40r: Carol Cooper. 41r: Ludovic Balland / © Ludovic Balland. All rights reserved. 41l: Luca de Salvia of Albert and Mildred Studio. 42: Ludovic Balland/ © Ludovic Balland. All rights reserved. 43: Sean Bird. A series of screenshots taken from my personal website, it uses a colourful, quirky – carnival approach, that engages and entertains the viewer. View it in all its glory at www.carnivalofsean.co.uk. 44: Laurence King Publishing. 45t: Four Brand Communications, Cadbury UK, Bournville, Birmingham, B30 2LU, T + 44 (0) 121 451 4646,www.fourbrands.co.uk. 45m and b: © 2009 Marc Austin and Paul Hale (Parc&Maul). 46: Katrin Schweigert / photography-image construction: Katrin Schweigert / layout: Katrin Schweigert / typography: Katrin Schweigert / © Katrin Schweigert (excluding 'Unity over Division, Hope over Despair, Solidarity over Self-interest' Amnesty International Report 2007 on the state of Human Rights). 47t: Astrid Stavro / Client: Art Directors Club of Europe / Art Direction: Astrid Stavro / Design: Richard Sarson, Ana Dominguez, Astrid Stavro. 47b: Marijke Cobbenhagen, invitation for the Netherlands Media Art Institute (NIMK) / Design by Cobbenhagen and Hendriksen. 48l: Lindsey Marshall. 48r: Lindsey Marshall. 49: Design: Grandpeople / Illustration: Grandpeople / Client: Oslo Architects Association. 50–51: Martin Woodtli. 52: Packaging Design by Bill Stewart / © 2007 Laurence King Publishing Ltd. 53t: Astrid Stavro, Travesias (collection of essays) / Client: Arcadia / Art direction: Astrid Stavro / Design: Astrid Stavro. 53b: Martin Woodtli. 54t: Lindsey Marshall &

Marc Austin. Images supplied by David Cardy George Maraziotis, *Muse*, 56 x 80 cm, pencils, acrylics and Indian ink on carton paper, created in Patras, Greece, 2008 for the purpose of my first personal exhibition *Inside* Peter Slight, illustration for SYSW Music Festival / © Peter Slight 2007 Tomas Bjornsson / www.tomasbjornsson.dk - tb@tomasbjornsson.dk Joel Millerchip, illustration by Joel Millerchip / www.mistermillerchip.com. 54b: Ed Fella. 56–57: © 2009 Marc Austin & Paul Hale (Parc&Maul). 58: Agency: Frost Design, Sydney, Australia. 60l: Peter Kent. 60r: Jean-Benoît Lévy/ street poster to advertise a theatre piece by Michel de Ghelderode, at the Theatre Marat/Sade in Basel / Photo: Stephan Meichtry / Design: Jean-Benoit Levy. www.and.ch / Agency: Studio AND / Client: Tino Krattiger/ Marat Sade / Serigraphie: Uldry. 61: Nicola Chang / Hong Kong Science Museum. 62t: Bunch Design / Agency: Cog 1. 62b: TutuTyutyunnik, 2008. 64: University of Falmouth / Phillip Skinner / Will Kinchin / Tom Probert / Jon Creighton-Griffiths. 65: Amirali Ghasemi for Parkingallery Studio / designed for a campaign to raise awareness about HIV in Asia / Published in the book: Intact/NL. 66: 37061169 Â© 2009 Jupiterimages Corporation. 67: 37061190 Â© 2009 Jupiterimages Corporation. 68l: John Seth Marshall. 68r: Lester Meachem. 69: Lester Meachem. 70: Lester Meachem. 71: Lester Meachem. 73: John Seth Marshall. 74: Martin Woodtli. 75: Martin Woodtli. 76: © Ludovic Balland. All rights reserved. 77: Lindsey Marshall. 78t: Design: Grandpeople / Illustrations: Grandpeople / Client: Bergen County Council. 78b: TutuTyutyunnik/ 2007. 79: Madelyn Postman / The National Spanish Jazz Orchestra (Orquesta Nacionak de Jazz de Espana – ONJAZZ) has roots in all eras and types of Spanish music, itself in turn influenced by everything from Moorish to American genres. Inspirations range from folk to classic jazz, big band to flamenco, all with a variety of instruments and famous guest composers. The identity echoes the same dynamism and eclecticism of the orchestra / Designed by Madelyn Postman of Madomat for Ramon Farran, director of ONJAZZ. 80t: All ethnic typography, copy, photography, lighting, styling and clothing, conceived, designed, produced and composed by Muiz Anwar. 80b: Sean Bird. 81: Design and illustration by Jason Munn/The Small Stakes. 82: Design and illustration by Jason Munn/The Small Stakes. 83: Sahra Mesgna, an exhibition poster designed to revamp the look of the 'Science and Art of Medicine Exhibition' at the Science Museum, London, entitled 'Blood and Guts'. 84: Joel Stone / The University of Bolton, 2008 / www.joelstone. co.uk. 85t: Illustration by Daniel Morgenstern, appeared in the weekend section of *Maariv*. 85b: Phillip Skinner. 86: 5077876 © Shutterstock images/Marek Slusarczyk. 87: Lindsey Marshall. 88l: Joshua Gidman. 88r: ATTAK • Powergestaltung, Red Ribbon Rock, 2007 / Media: poster / Client: Red Ribbon Rock. 89: ATTAK • Powergestaltung, bART Take Off, 2007 / Media: poster / Client: bART/platform voor actuele kunsten. 90–93: Design: Grandpeople / Illustration: Grandpeople / Client: Hybris Records. 94: Agency: DDB London / Photographer: Giles Revell @ Stella Pye / Modelmaker: Andy Knight. 96t: Joshua Gidman. 96b: Lindsey Marshall. 97: Getty Images/The Bridgeman Art Library. 99: Asbjorn G Andvig. 100tl: Ian Pollock. 100tr: Beth Walker. 100b: Claes Oldenburg, *Soft Switches*, 1964. Vinyl and Dacron, 47 x 47 inches (119.4 x 119.4 cm). The Nelson-Atkins Museum of Art, Kansas City, Missouri. Gift of the Chapin Family in memory of Susan Chapin Buckwalter, 65-29. Photograph by Jamison Miller. 101tl: Mary Davis, Crop Pool 2, digital enhanced gicleé print, 41.5cm x 39.5 cm U.V. inks.101tr: Lindsey Marshall. 102: Phillip Skinner. 103t: Designed and illustrated by Jason Munn/The Small Stakes. 103b: 12009371 Â© 2009 Jupiterimages Corporation. 104: © 2009 Dave Colton. 105t and b: Lester Meachem. 106: Sean Bird, a self-promotional piece taking words, colours and influences to reveal what goes on in my head. This was used for the basis of my website which you can view in all its glory at www.carnivalofsean.co.uk. 107tr: Chris Bolton, typographic illustration / Page layout: Pekka Toivanen / Photography: Jonas Vuorinen. 107bl: Project: ASCII Animation, 2003. Still from 'Eye, Reading – Loop' for 'Reading Department' commissioned by Alsop Architects, London, and

exhibited as part of the Bienal de Valencia (2003) www.flat33.com.
107br: 6921917 © iStockphoto.com/Frank van den Bergh. 108tl: Getty
Images / Iconica / Peter Cade. 108tr: Getty Images / Stone / Daniel Klajmic.
108b: Aarefa Tayabji. 109: Amirali Ghasemi / Parkingallery Studio. 110: Jon
Rhodes. 111: Designed and illustrated by Jason Munn/The Small Stakes.
112: Zane K.J. Manasco – Photophilliac-inc. 113: Lester Meachem.
114: Phillip Skinner. 115t: ℗ & © 2004 Dynamic Entertainment Ltd.
115b: © 2003 Shady Records/Aftermath Entertainment/Interscope
Records. 116l: Client: Gianfranco Bösch, Basel / Photo-Graphic: Franz
Werner, Providence, Rhode Island, USA / Graphic Design: Jean-Benoît
Lévy / Agency: Studio AND / www.and.ch. 116r: Photo: Pierre-Yves
Goavec / Design: Jean-Benoit Levy. / Agency: Studio AND / Client: Magic
Theatre, San Francisco / www.and.ch. 117: Image courtesy of The
Advertising Archives. 118–119: Zane K.J. Manasco – Photophilliac-inc.
120: Inksurge. 122–123: Bunch Design. 124tl: 6096843 ©iStockphoto.
com/Toutoudaki. 124tr: 10835962 Â© 2009 Jupiterimages Corporation.
124b: 84238954 Â© 2009 Jupiterimages Corporation. 125t: Amirali
Ghasemi/Parkingallery Studio. 125b: Sean Bird, a proposed leaflet design,
which was never used, for Wolverhampton Art Gallery. It advertises a newly
opened collections resources centre. The design focuses on what you
would experience as a visitor. An unconventional, surprising approach.
126: Ludovic Balland Office. 127: Bunch Design / Client: Rob Star.
128t: Selina Yuk Tzang Pan. 128b: Image courtesy of The Advertising
Archives. 129: Amirali Ghasemi for Parkingallery Studio / Client: Azad Art
Gallery. 130tr: Robert Horne / Photography taken from SHOUT, the
showcase of winning work (design and print and use of material), published
each year by the Robert Horne Group / Photography by: Guy Farrow /
www.roberthorne.co.uk. 130l and b: Lindsey Marshall (four images).
131: Chris Bolton, design and custom typography. 132: Karl Martin
Saetren. 133l: Lester Meachem.133r: Art Director: Adam Rix / Designer:
Adam Rix / Copywriter: Simon Griffin / Photographer: Antony Crook /
Illustrator: Rory Sutherland. 134–135: Chris Bolton, design and illustration.
136tl: Beth Walker. 136tr: Design: Grandpeople / Illustrations: Grandpeople
/ Client: Kompakt Records. 136b: Ed Fella, Silk Screen Print, 1963 / This
piece was done as a holiday promotion for several art reps at New Centre
Studios in Detroit. It combines Art Deco lettering and forms with the then
current 'Op Art' style. 137: Phillip Skinner. 139t: Elena Proskurova / face of
the lady from iStock.com istockphoto.com/iconofenic / elenaproskuurova.
blogspot.com. 139b: ATTAK • Powergestaltung, Dirt Ollies, 2007 / Media:
Magazinespread / editorial / Text: Scott Bourne / Photography: Pontus Aly,
Alexander Basile & Bertrand Trichet / Client: Bold Publishing/Reload
Magazine. 140t: Gareth Tsang. 140b: ATTAK • Powergestaltung, Opening
MAW Antwerpen, 2008 / Media: Poster / Client: MEN_at_WORK.
141: Luca de Salvia / Illustration: A, Whitehurst. 142: Courtesy & © Coca-
Cola Company. 143: Four Brand Communications, Cadbury UK, Bournville,
Birmingham, B30 2LU, T + 44 (0) 121 451 4646, www.fourbrands.co.uk.
144–145: John Clementson / Client: Carlin Production Music/Destiny Music
/ Job: CD Cover / Art Director: Paul Kinane / Media: Acrylic on Board /
Photography by John Seth Marshall. 146: Josef Müller-Brockmann,
Protégez l'enfant!, 1953 / poster for Automobile-Club de Suisse, Museum
für Gestaltung, Zürich, Poster Collection. 148: Grandpeople, design and
illustrations. 149t: Lester Meachem / Photography by Lindsey Marshall.
149bl: Lindsey Marshall. 149br: Lindsey Marshall. 150t: John Seth Marshall.
150b: Lindsey Marshall. 151t: © R Kuncyusz, this typographic image is
constructed using anonymous blog text sourced from http://beijingorbust.
com (author unknown), with help from Uwriu Ewrwer and his Voronoi
algorithm for processing. 151b: Sahra Mesgna, *Emotions on the Subway*
allows us to peer through a train carriage and engage with characters
expressing various emotions as they embark on their journey.
152l: © Annika Biitter, Semester 5th and instructor Uli Janssen,
Kunstschule Wandsbeck, Germany / Part of an outdoor-advertising-
campaign for an online ticket and event-portal in city lights, billboards and

buses. 152t: Amirali Ghasemi for Parkingallery Studio / Photographer:
Shabnam Zera'ati / Client: Parkingallery Studio. 152br: Gloria K. Fiero,
Landmarks in Humanities, courtesy and © 2009 The McGraw-Hill
Companies, Inc. All rights reserved. Designed and produced by Laurence
King Publishing Ltd. 153tl and tr: John Seth Marshall. 153bl and br: © 2009
Marc Austin & Paul Hale (Parc&Maul). 154l: Jean-Benoît Lévy / Purpose:
Invitational poster/ Street poster on occasion of the 700 years of Switzerland:
for a Switzerland with engagement in environmental conscience /
Photomontage: Jean-Pascal Imsand / Concept and design: Jean-Benoît
Lévy. www.and.ch / Serigraphie: Uldry. 154r: Ed Fella. 155t: John Seth
Marshall. 155b: John Seth Marshall photograph, manipulated by Lester
Meachem. 156: ATTAK • Powergestaltung, Paleiskwartier, 2005 / Media:
Poster / Client: Avans Hogeschool/ AKV St. Joost. 157tl: Courtesy Joyce
Walsh Macario. 157ml: 000007065762 ©iStockphoto.com/Roberto A
Sanchez. 157mr: 78182812 Â© 2009 Jupiterimages Corporation.
157r: Sahra Mesgna, when one is deep in thought generally their eyes tend
to glance upwards. The idea behind the Look up Urban Movement was to
encourage and inspire people living in the city. 158–159: Nicola Chang /
Hong Kong Science Museum. 160: Design: Browns / Project: One of three
posters to promote artist Jonathan Ellery's exhibition Unrest at the Wapping
Project / www.brownsdesign.com www.brownseditions.com. 162: United
States Postal Service © 2001 The Record. All rights reserved. © 2005
USPS. 163: Martin Woodtli. 164: Lindsey Marshall. 165: Robert Horne /
Photography taken from SHOUT, the showcase of winning work (design
and print and use of material), published each year by the Robert Horne
Group / Photography by: Guy Farrow / www.roberthorne.co.uk.
165b: 3167858 Â© 2009 Jupiterimages Corporation. 166–168: Robert
Horne / Photography by: John Seth Marshall. 168r: 82150852 Â© 2009
Jupiterimages Corporation. 168b: Design: Grandpeople / Illustrations:
Grandpeople / Client: Bergen County Council. 169t: 79967387 Â© 2009
Jupiterimages Corporation. 169m: Robert Horne, dps from book 50
Fantastic Years of Chromolux / Photography by John Seth Marshall.
169b: Karl Martin Saetren / Painting by Marius Martinussen / Design and
photography by KalleGraphics. 170t: Michael W. Neal. 170b: © The China
Engraving and Printing Works. 171: Art Director: Adam Rix / Designer:
Adam Rix / Copywriter: Simon Griffin / Illustrator: Emma Morton.
172–174: Lester Meachem. 175: ATTAK • Powergestaltung, Jazz
Werkplaats, 2006 / Media: Flyer / Client: Jazz Werkplaats Den Bosch.
176t and bl: Lindsey Marshall / Photography: John Seth Marshall.
176br: Created and produced by Helen Shillabeer. 177bl: 11926142 Â©
2009 Jupiterimages Corporation. 177br: 68172091 Â© 2009 Jupiterimages
Corporation. 178: photo by Atelier Tom Blaess. 181: © 2009 Marc Austin &
Paul Hale (Parc&Maul). 182: Omega!The KidPhoepnix / Bunch Design
183: Ten do Ten/Bunch Design / Marantha Wilson/Bunch Design / Hideki
Nakajima/Bunch Design / Animated fun –fur "B" by Marian Bantjes/Bunch
Design / Nick Sims www.nick-sims.com/Bunch Design / Michael Pope,
design was inspired by a cubmission call from Bunch, a design firm based
in London. Artists were invited to bastasdize the current logo and identity
piece, into a unique expression. This was my take. – MP/Bunch Design /
Julien Robust, I work alone, for this work I used a ghost of Pac Man, Pinky
and I credit the idea man Toru Iwatani and Namco/Bunch Design / Revenge
is sweet/Bunch Design. 184–185: Bunch Design.

Index